PAT METHENY w/CHRISTIAN M...
DAY TRIP/TOKY...

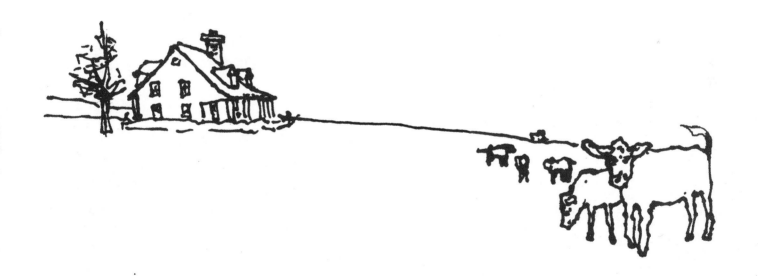

Music transcriptions by Masa Takahashi

ISBN 978-1-61780-542-4

7777 W. BLUEMOUND RD. P.O. BOX 13819 MILWAUKEE, WI 53213

For all works contained herein:
Unauthorized copying, arranging, adapting, recording, Internet posting, public performance,
or other distribution of the printed music in this publication is an infringement of copyright.
Infringers are liable under the law.

Visit Hal Leonard Online at
www.halleonard.com

DAY TRIP

- 4 SON OF THIRTEEN
- 19 AT LAST YOU'RE HERE
- 36 LET'S MOVE
- 53 SNOVA
- 64 CALVIN'S KEYS
- 79 IS THIS AMERICA?
- 86 WHEN WE WERE FREE
- 101 DREAMING TREES
- 110 THE RED ONE
- 120 DAY TRIP

TOKYO DAY TRIP

140   **TROMSØ**
157   **TRAVELING FAST**
186   **INORI**
194   **BACK ARM & BLACKCHARGE**
212   **THE NIGHT BECOMES YOU**

222   **Guitar Notation Legend**

Son of Thirteen

By Pat Metheny

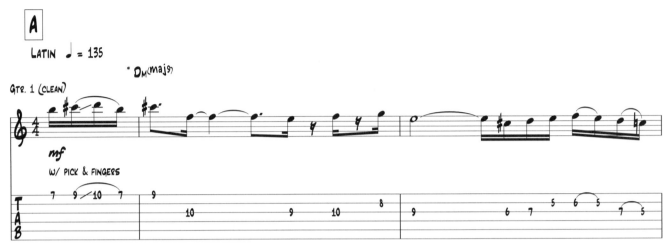

*Chord symbols reflect overall harmony.

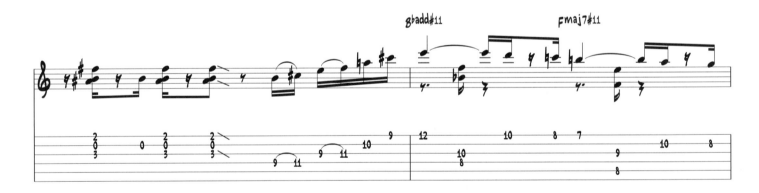

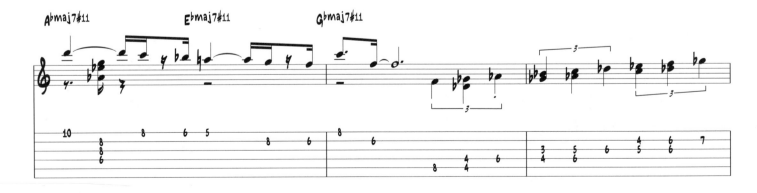

Copyright © 2008 Pat Meth Music Corp.
All Rights Reserved   Used by Permission

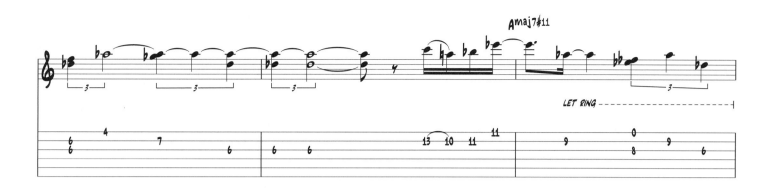
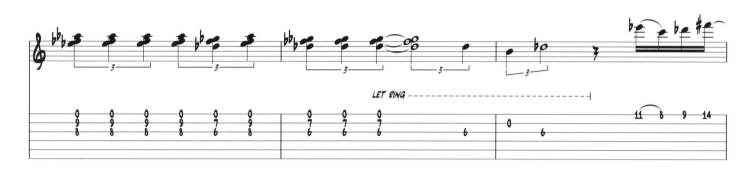
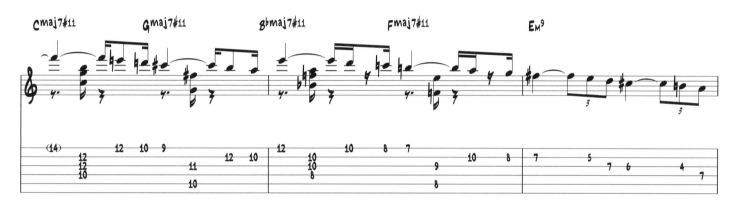
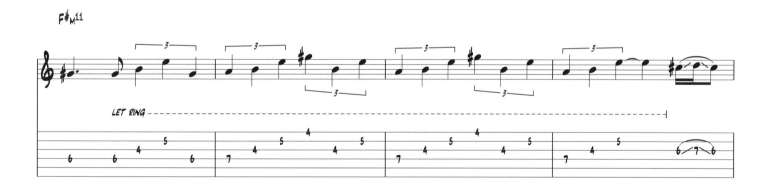
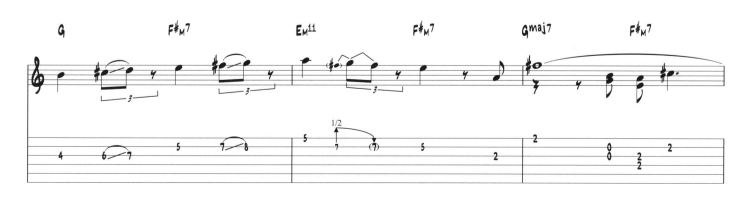

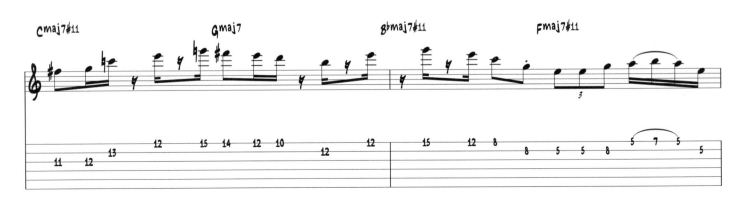

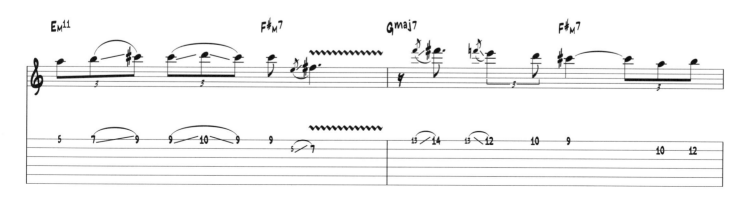

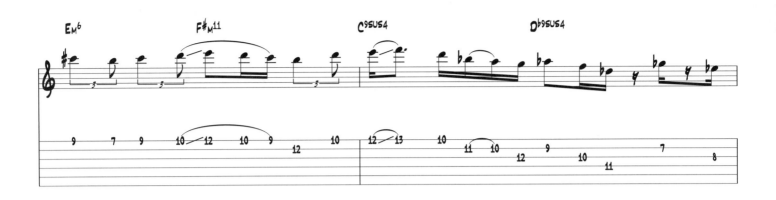

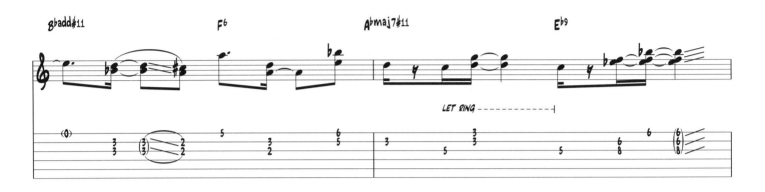

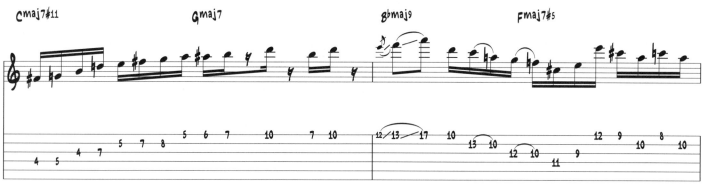

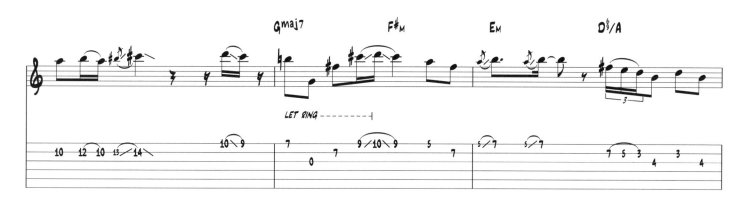

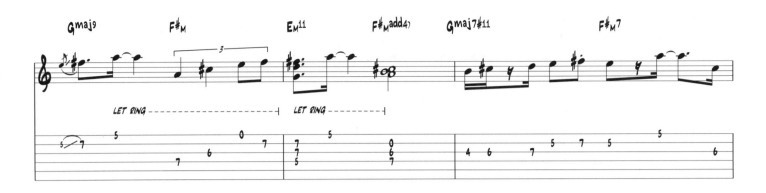
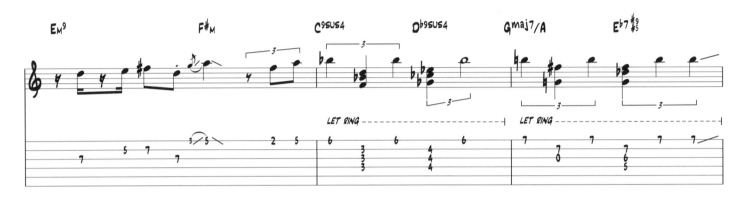

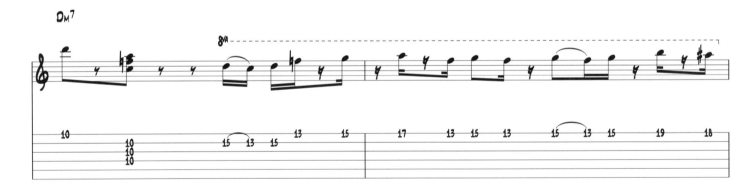
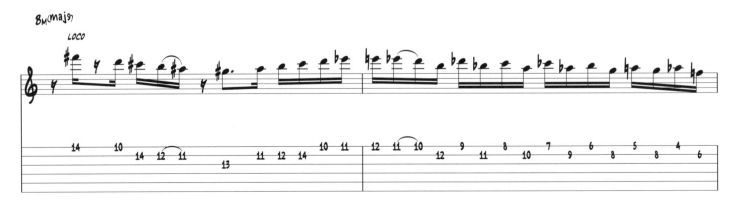

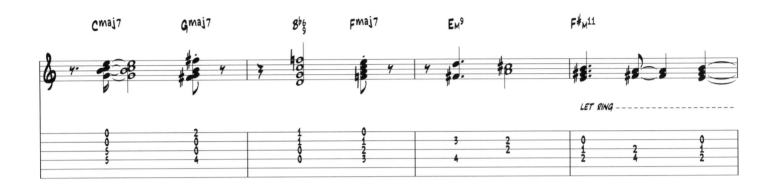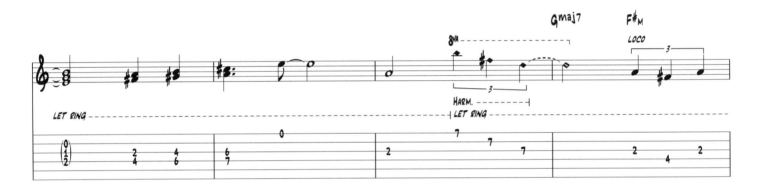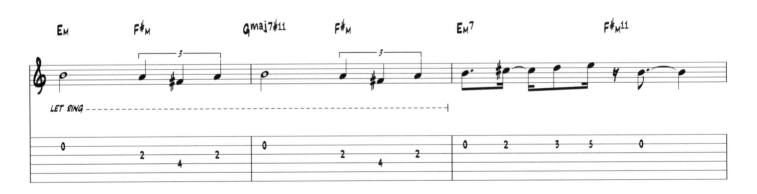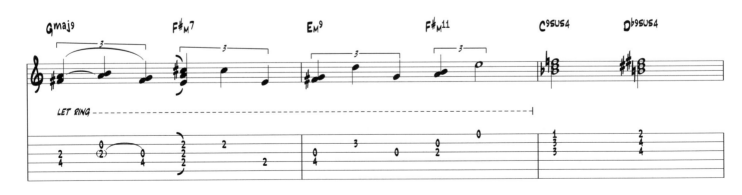

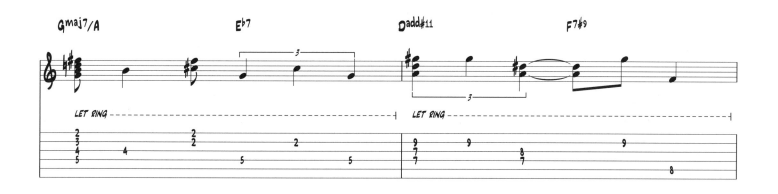
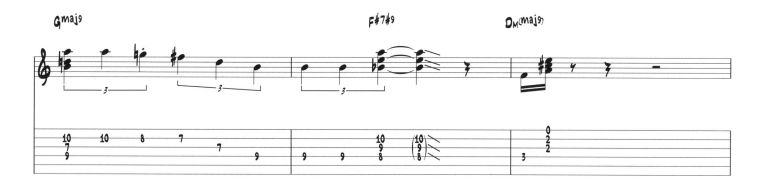
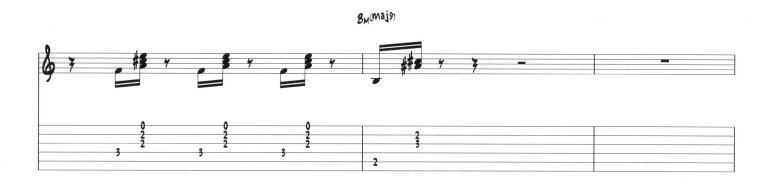
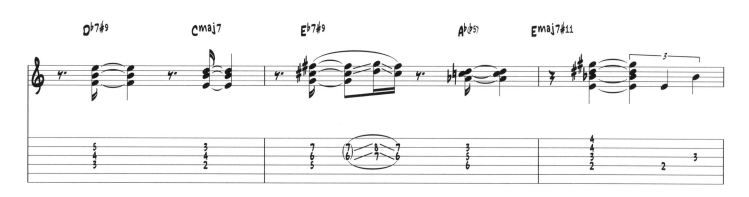
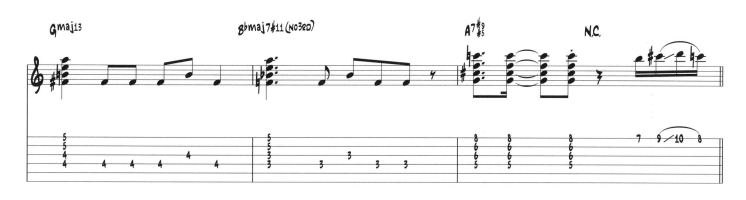

At Last You're Here
By Pat Metheny

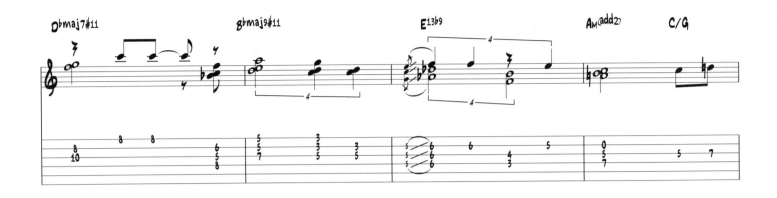

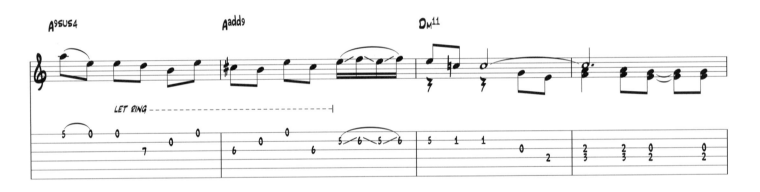

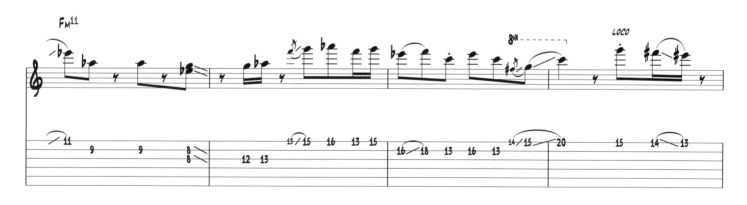

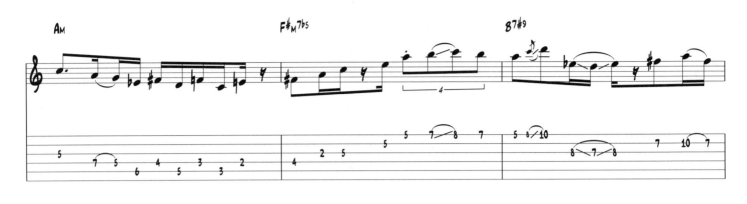

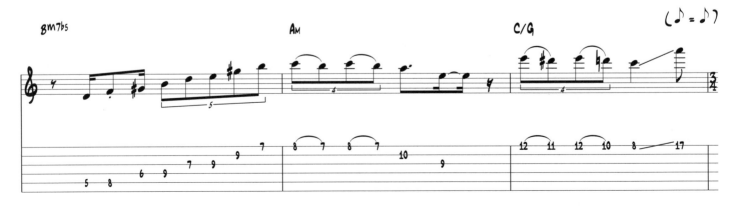

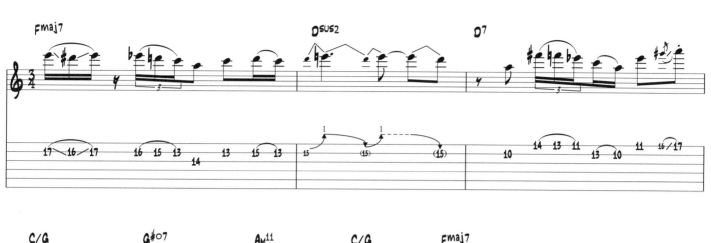
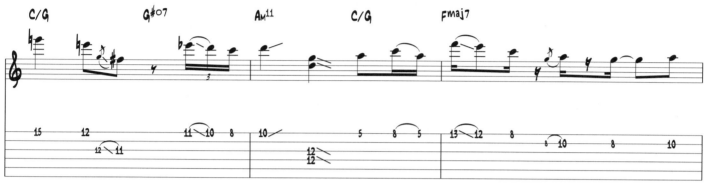

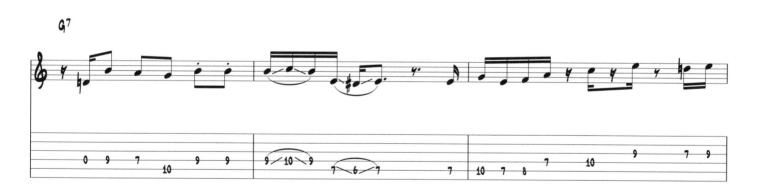

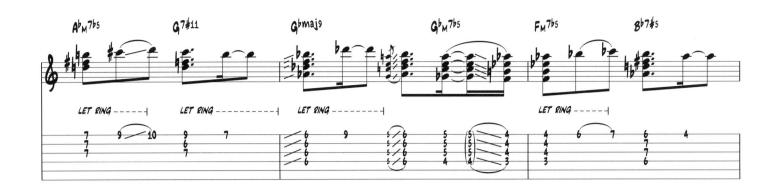

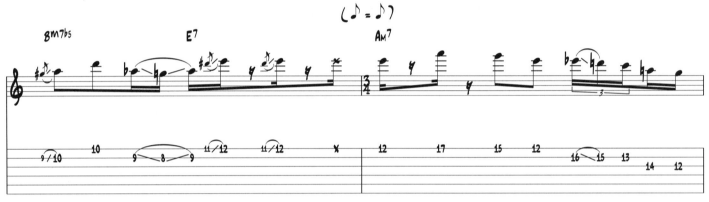
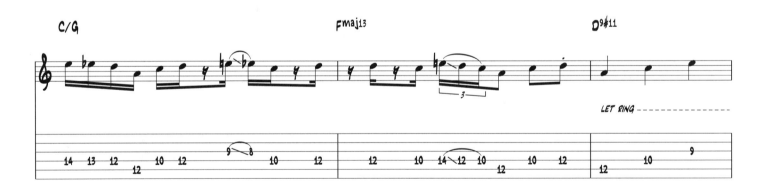
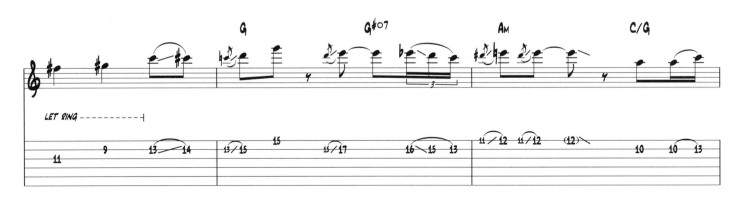

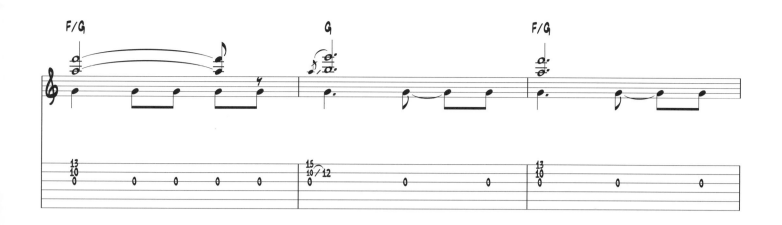
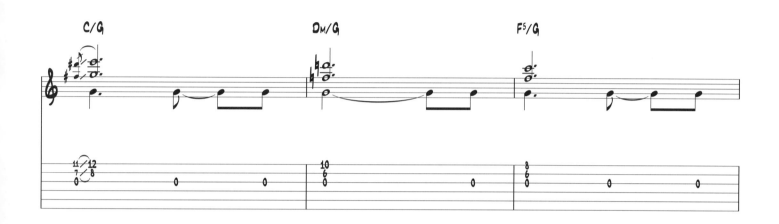
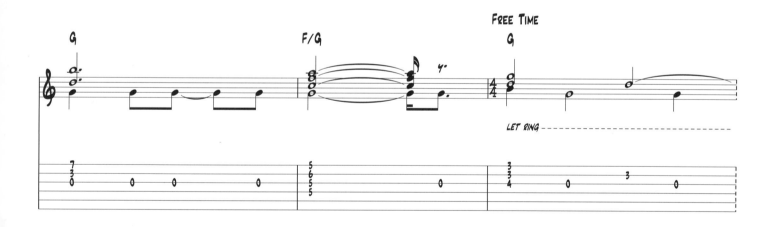
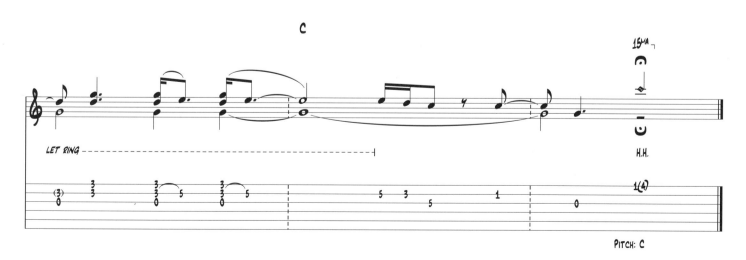

Let's Move
By Pat Metheny

37

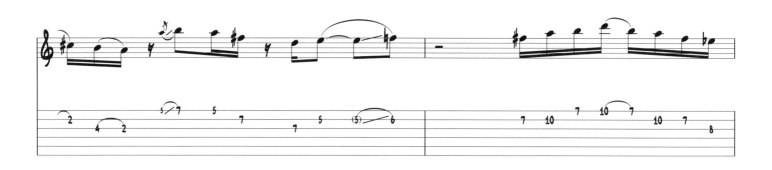

D♭7sus4

41

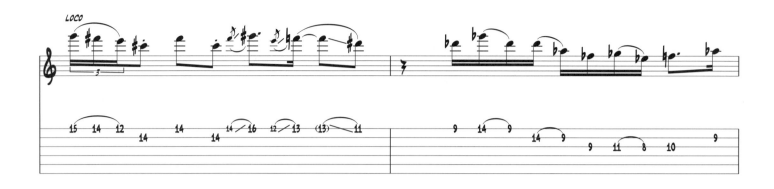

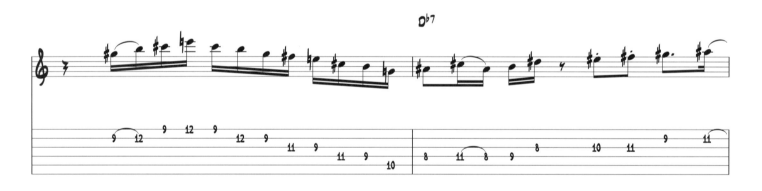
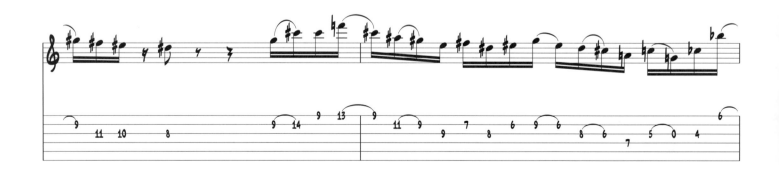

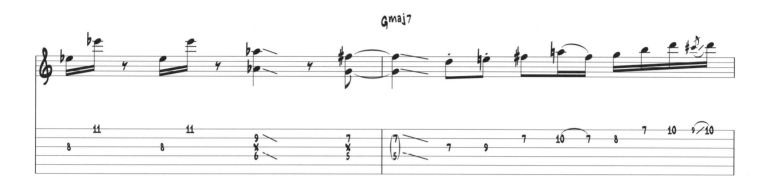
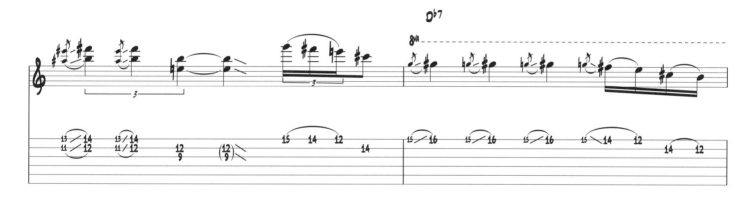
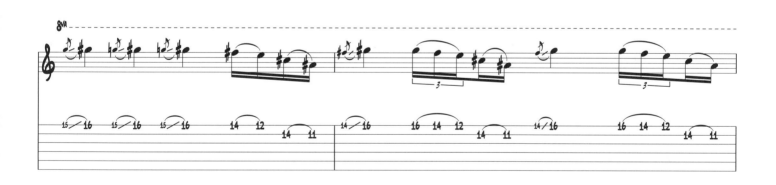
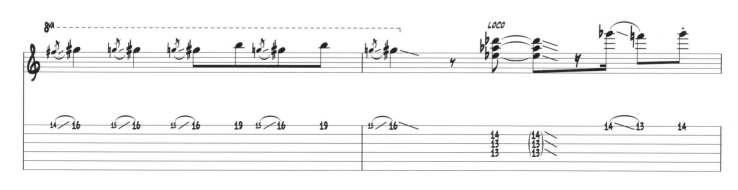

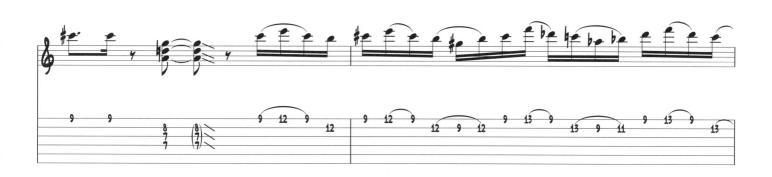
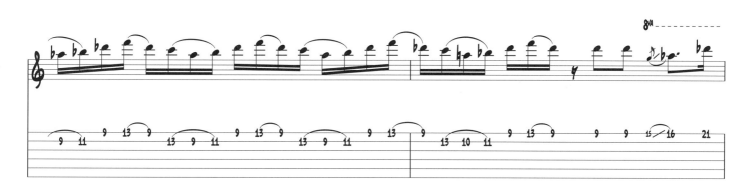

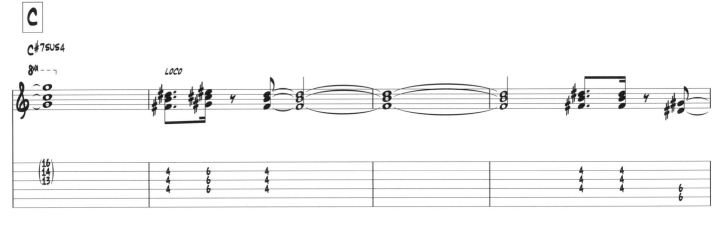

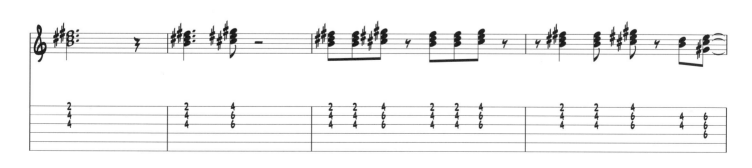

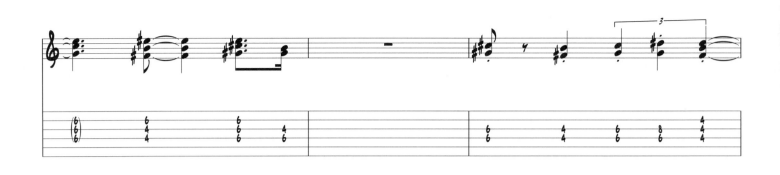
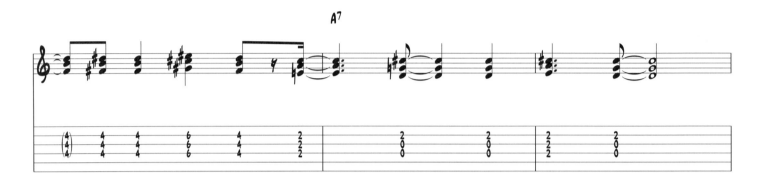
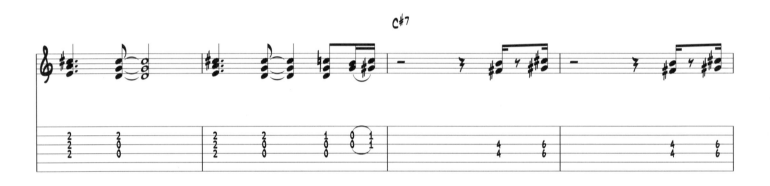
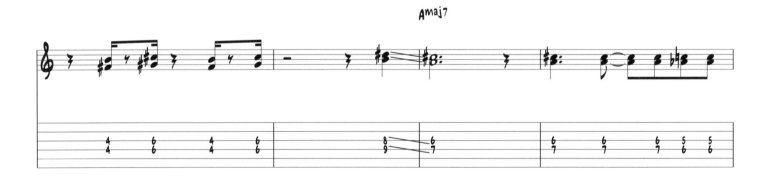

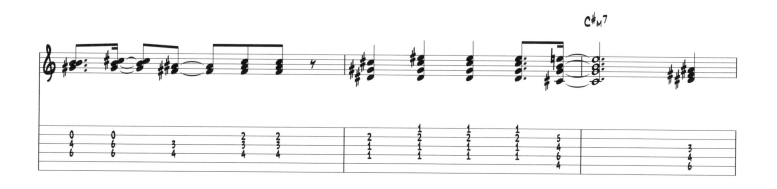

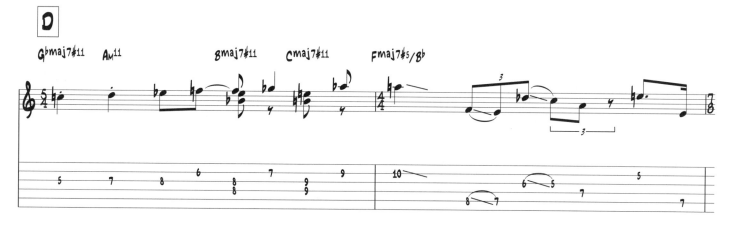

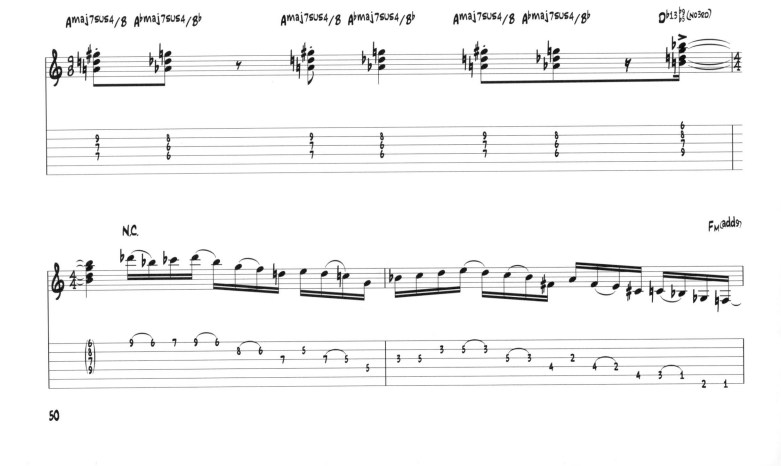

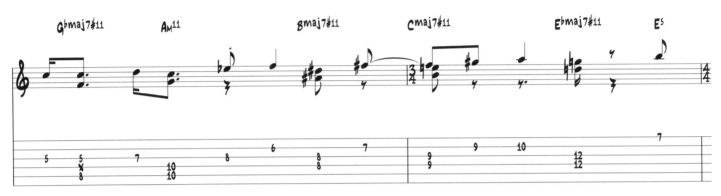
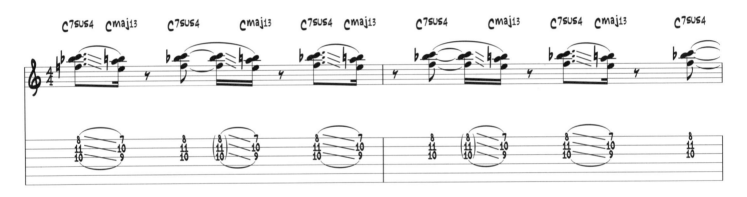

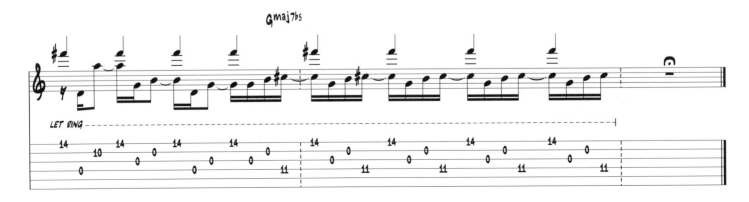

Snova

By Pat Metheny

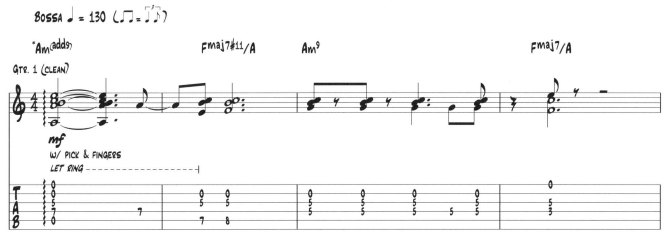

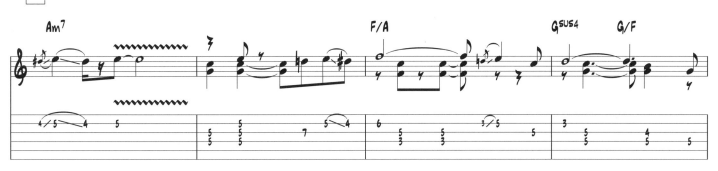

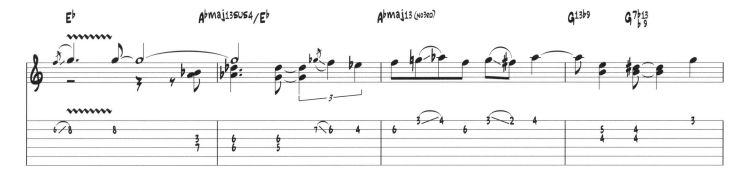

Copyright © 2008 Pat Meth Music Corp.
All Rights Reserved   Used by Permission

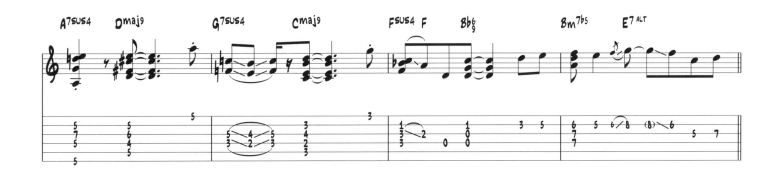

*Played behind the beat.

**As before

***As before

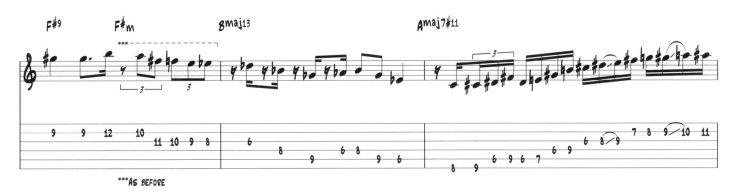

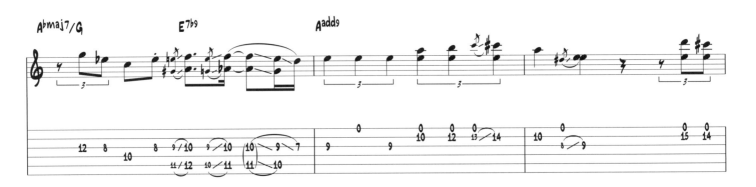

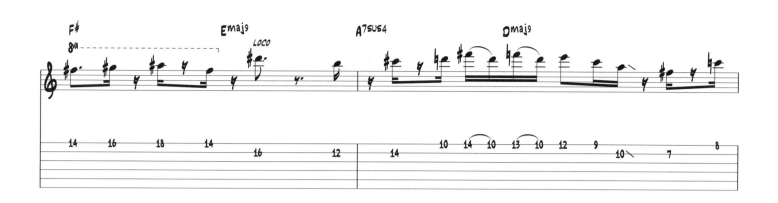
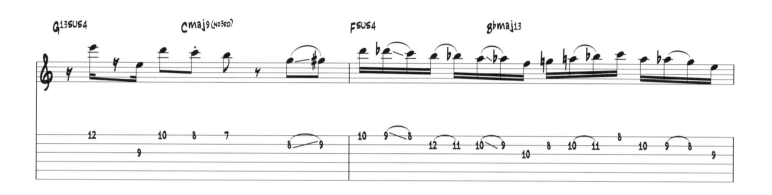

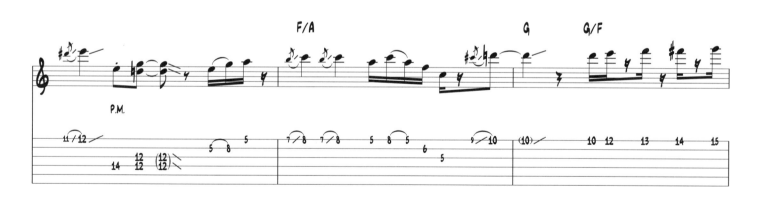
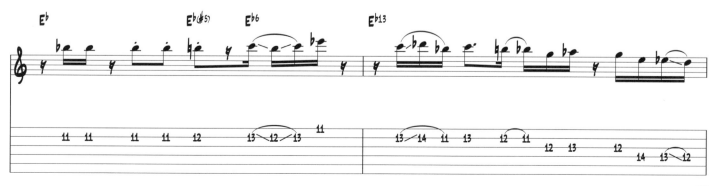

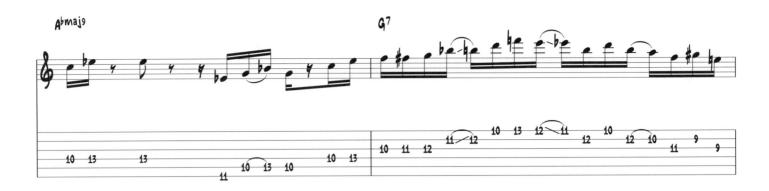

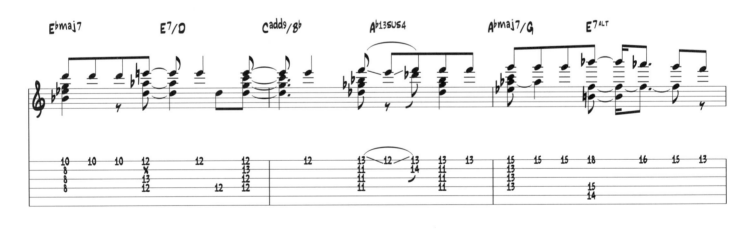

Calvin's Keys
By Pat Metheny

*Chord symbols reflect overall harmony.

Copyright © 2008 Pat Meth Music Corp.
All Rights Reserved Used by Permission

*Played behind the beat.

**As before ***As before

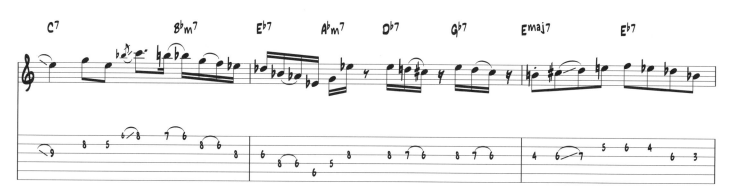

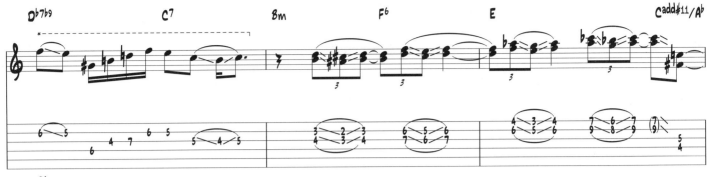

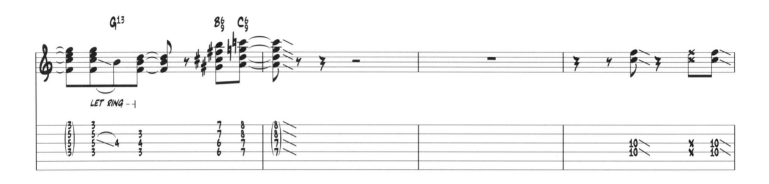
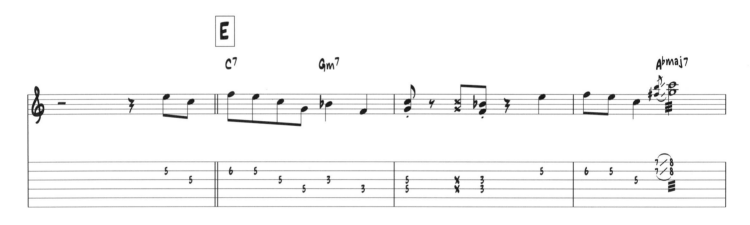

*Chord symbol reflects basic harmony.

*As before

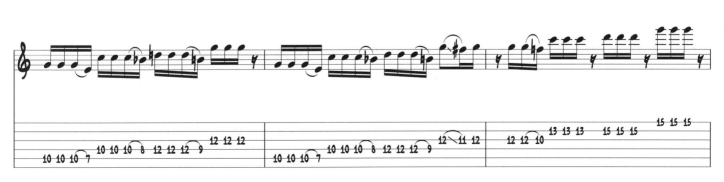

BEGIN FADE

FADE OUT

Is This America?

By Pat Metheny

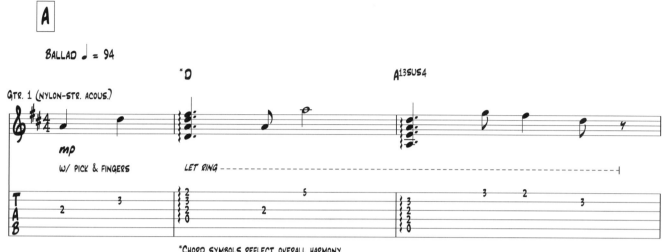

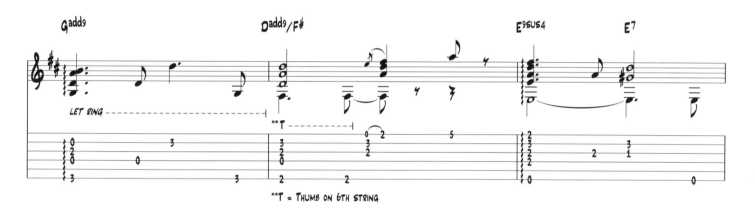

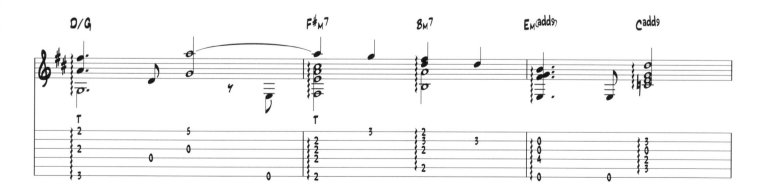

Copyright © 2008 Pat Meth Music Corp.
All Rights Reserved   Used by Permission

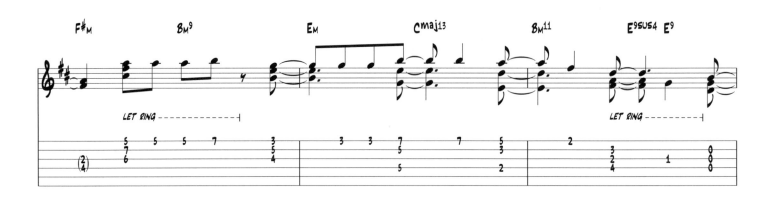

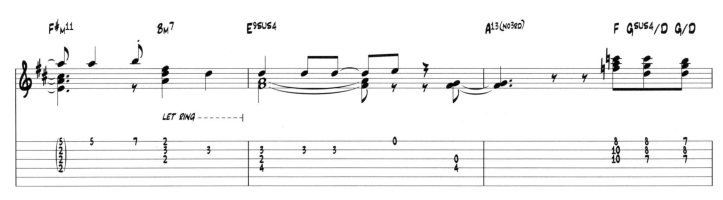

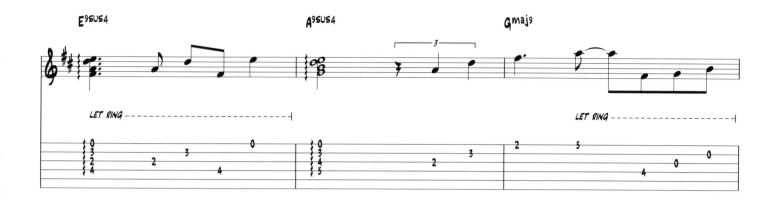

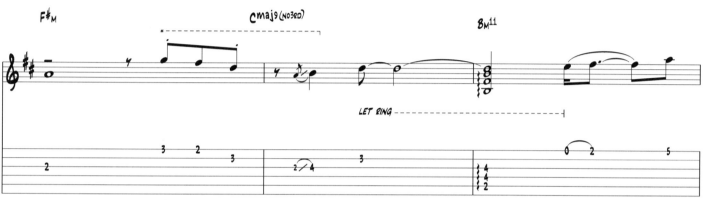

*Played behind the beat.

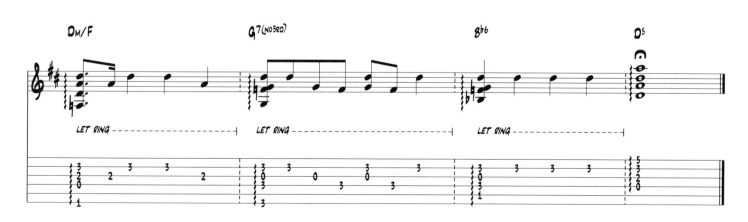

When We Were Free
By Pat Metheny

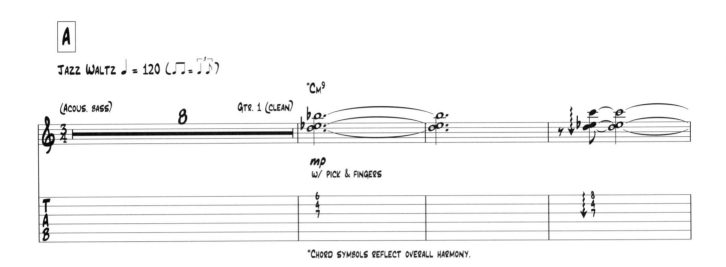

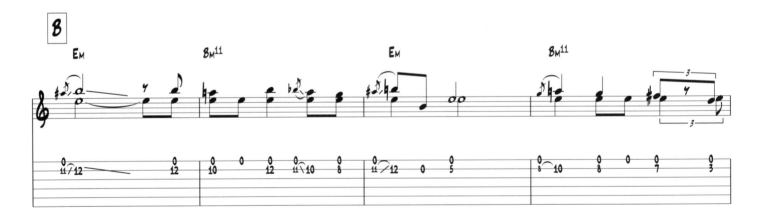

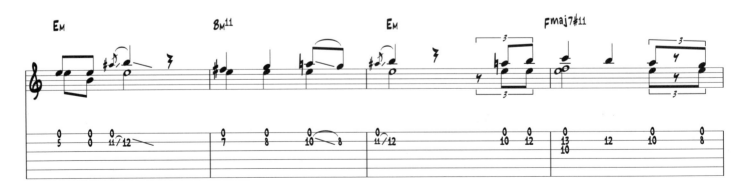

*Refers to open E string only.

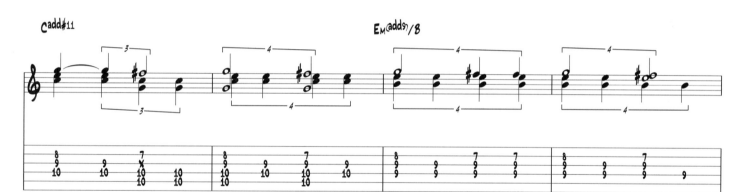
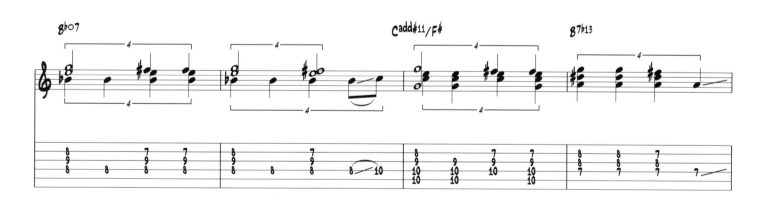
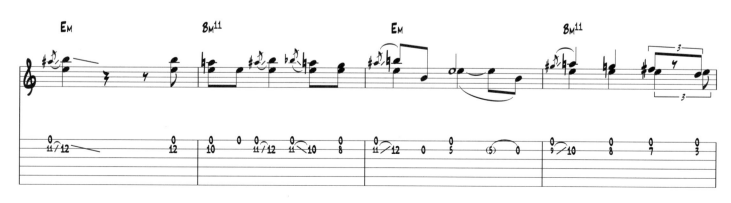

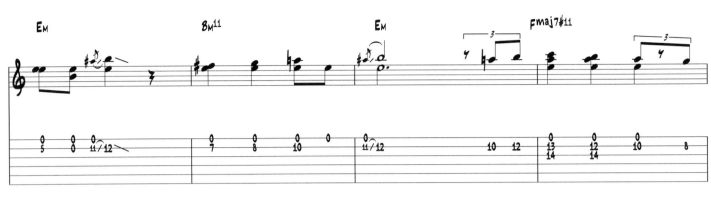
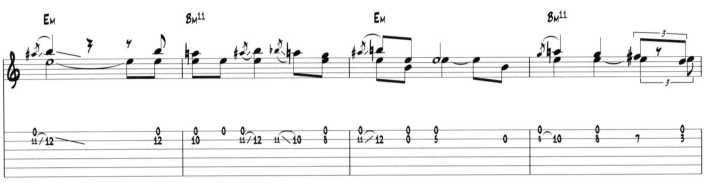
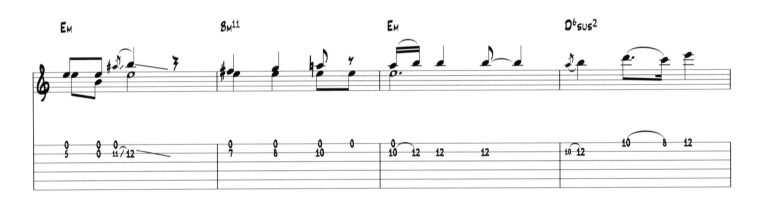
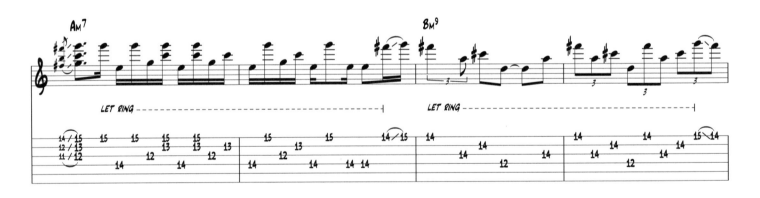
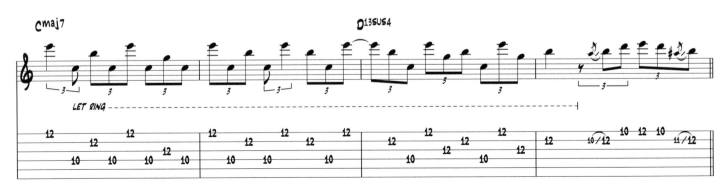

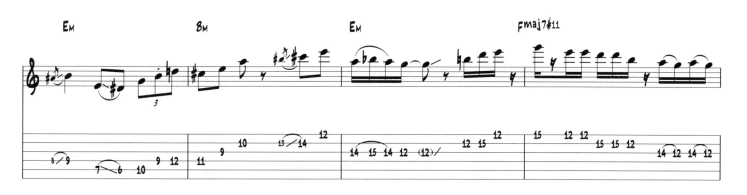

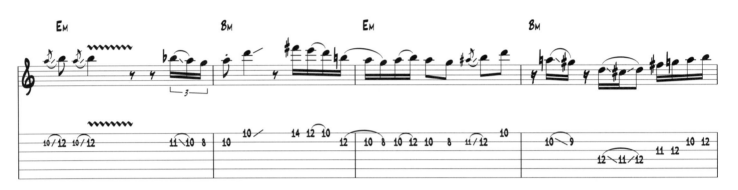

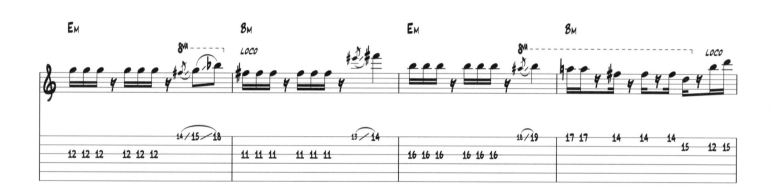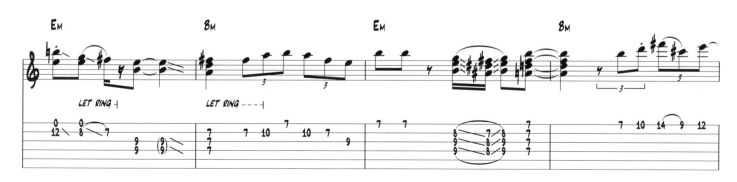

*Played behind the beat.

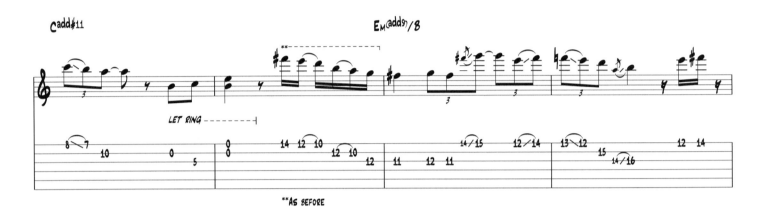

**As before

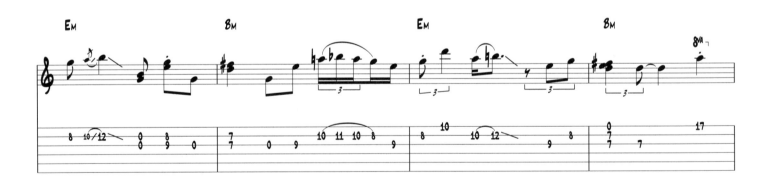

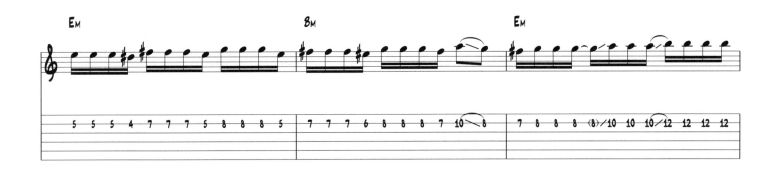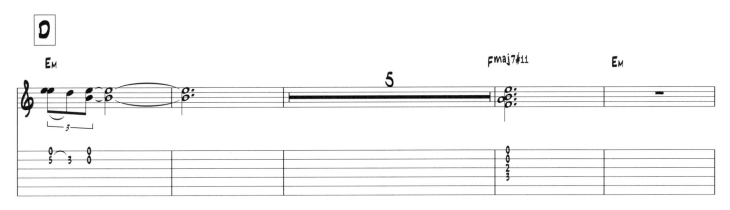

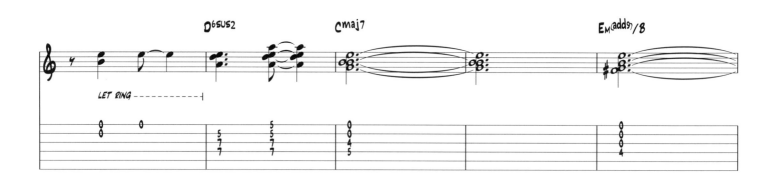
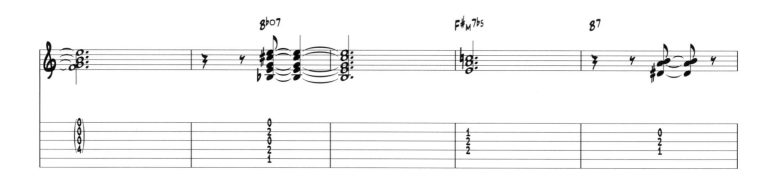
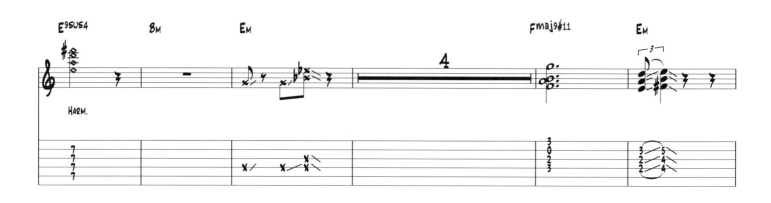
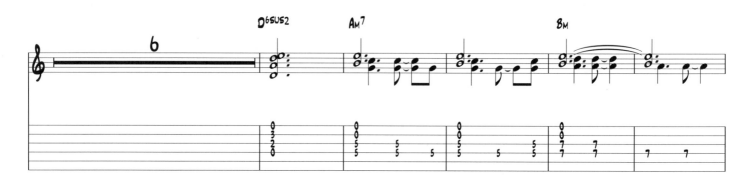

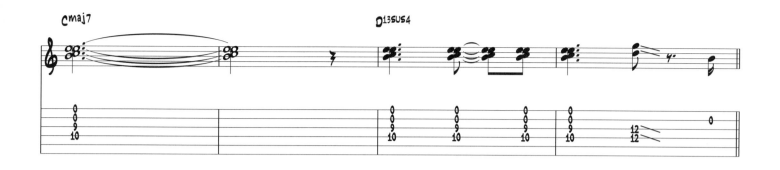

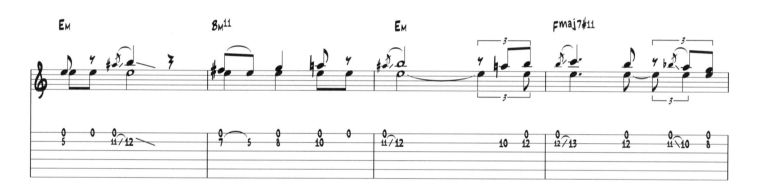

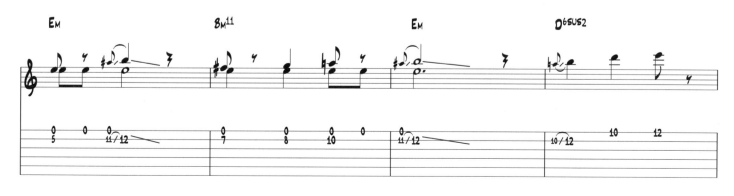

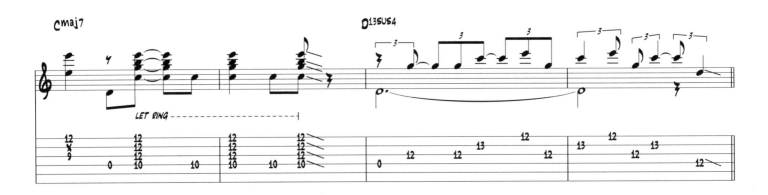

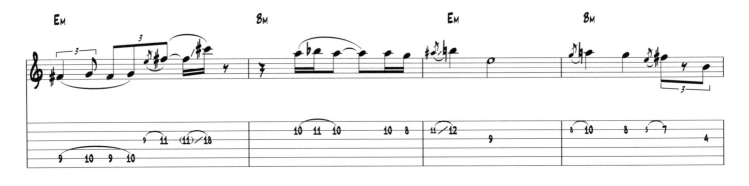

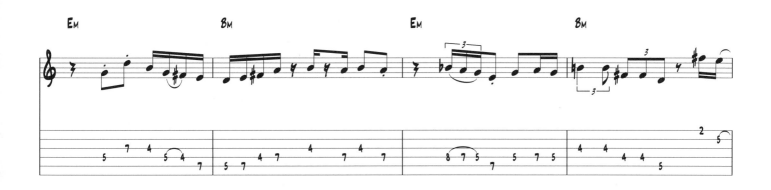

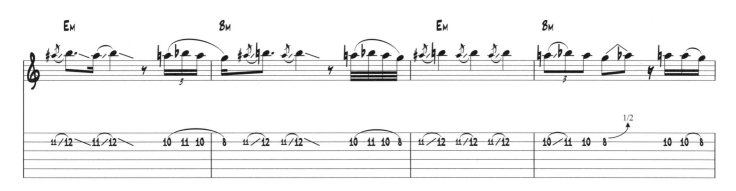
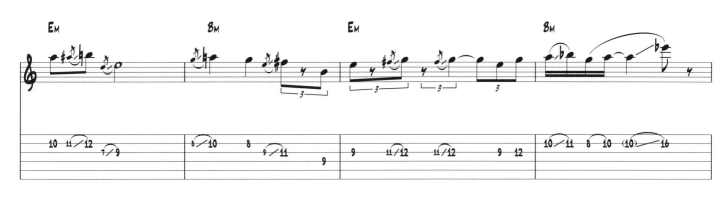

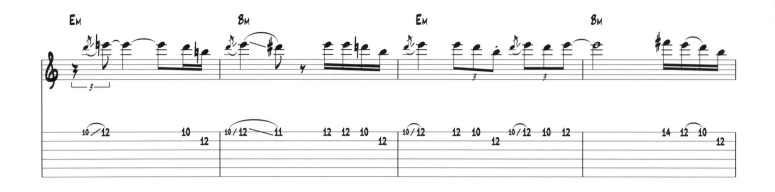

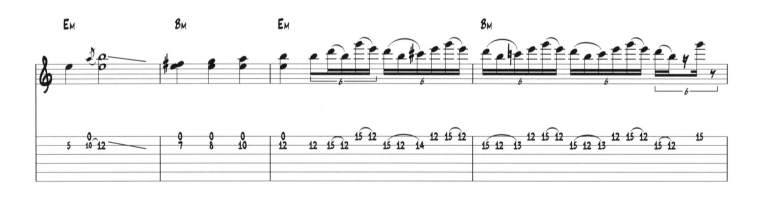
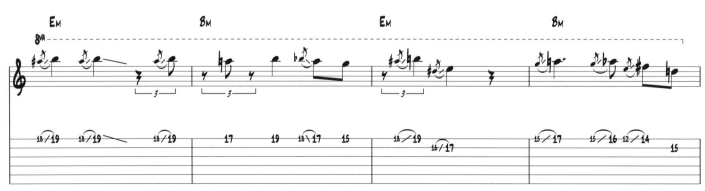

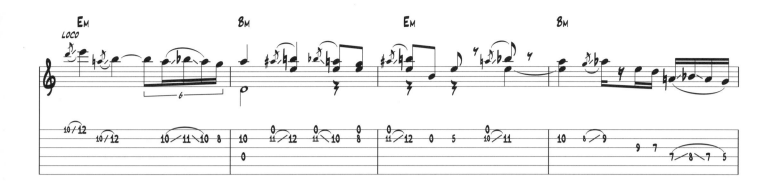
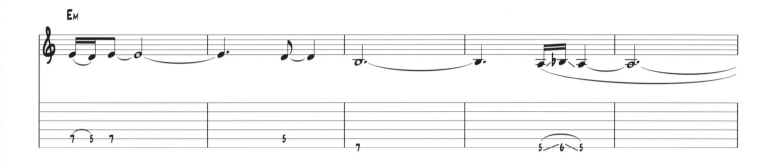
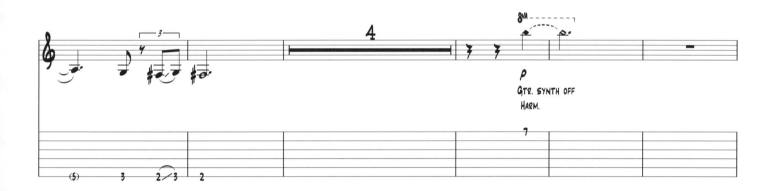
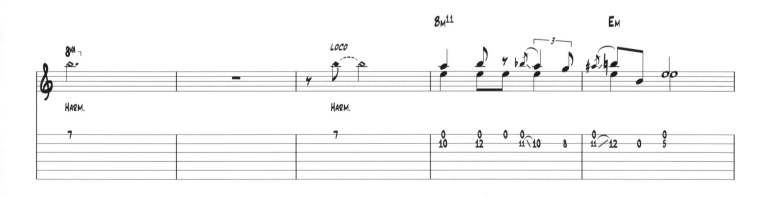
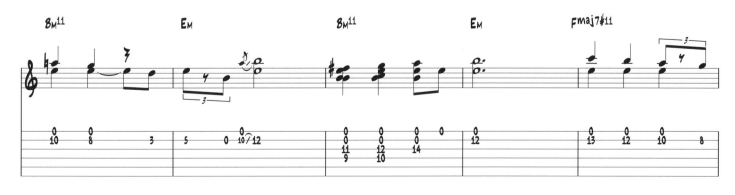

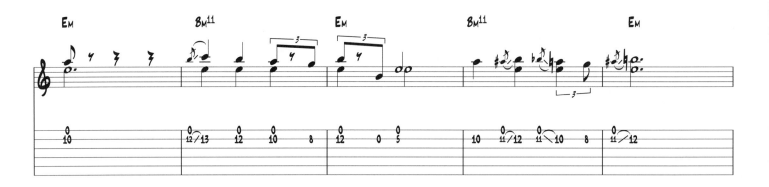
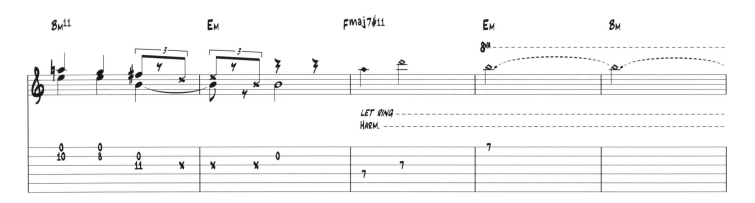
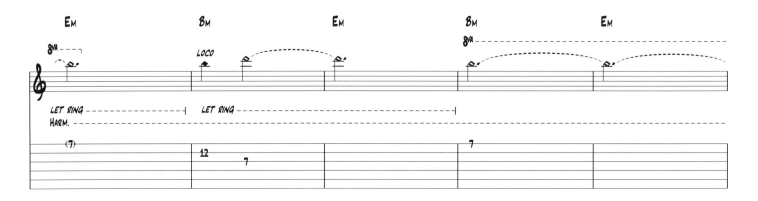
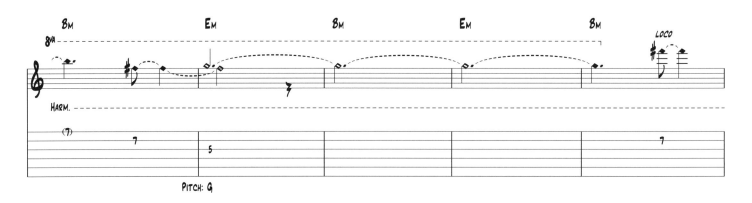
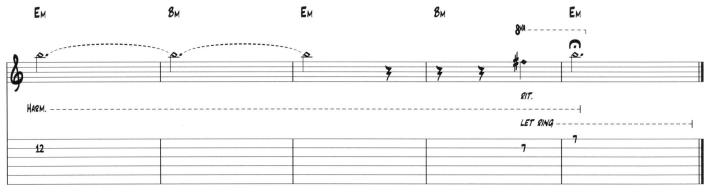

Dreaming Trees

By Pat Metheny

Copyright © 2008 Pat Meth Music Corp.
All Rights Reserved Used by Permission

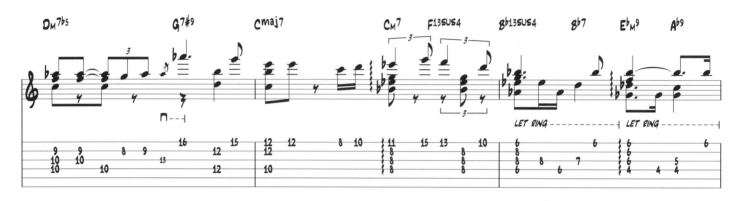

*Played behind the beat.

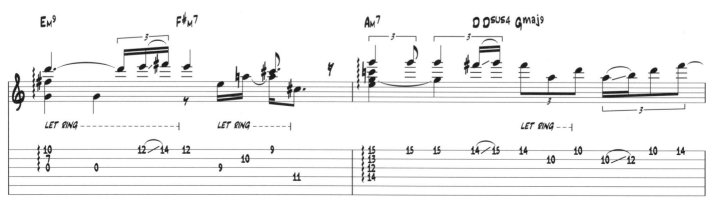

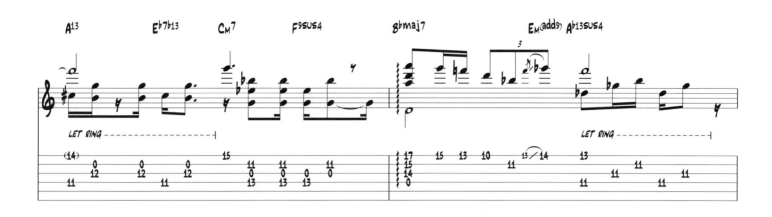
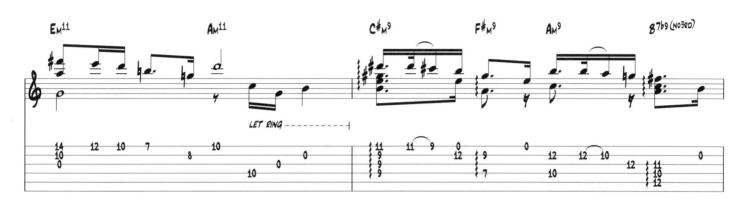
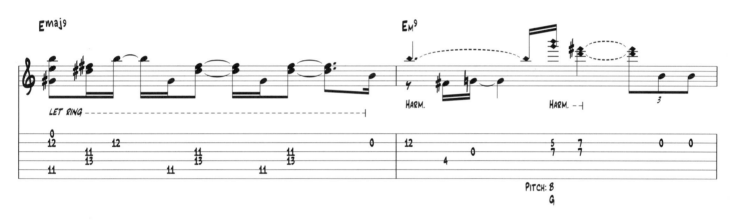
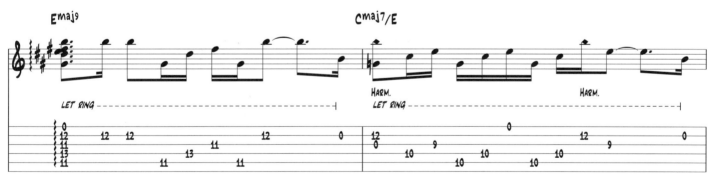

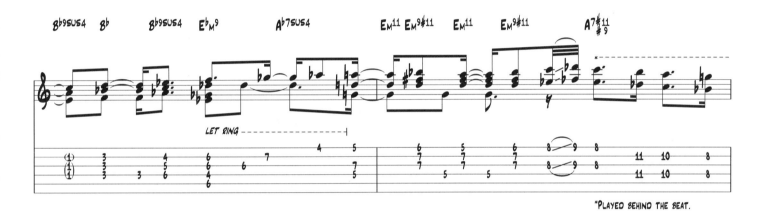

*Played behind the beat.

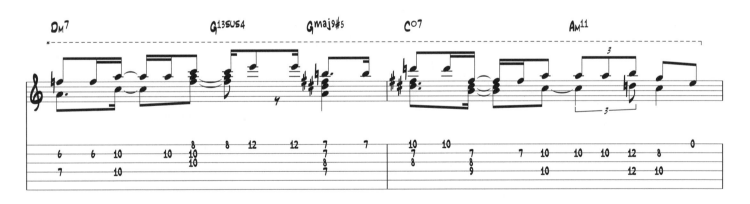
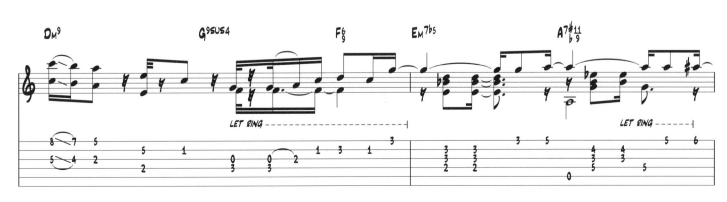

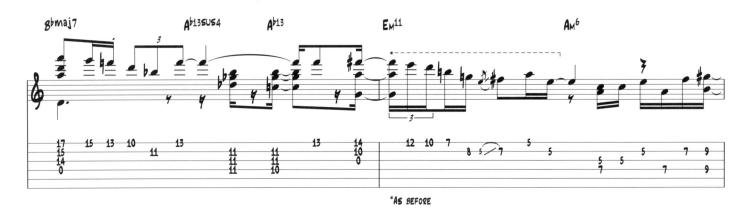

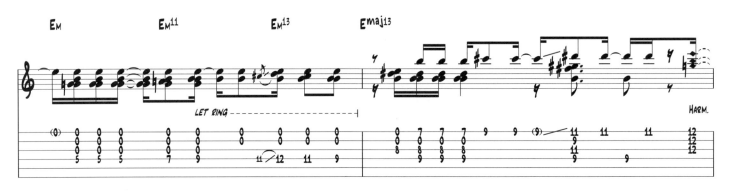

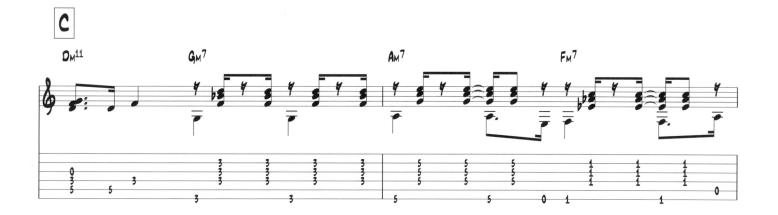
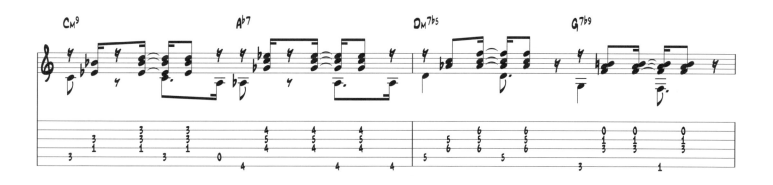

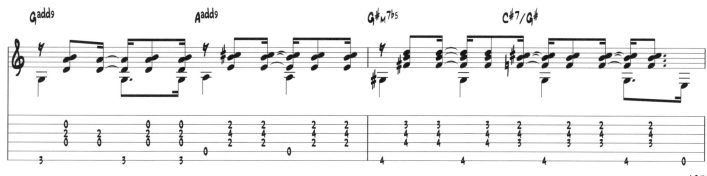

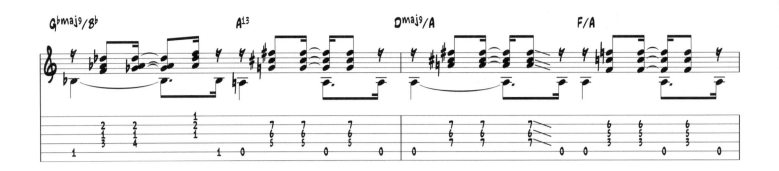
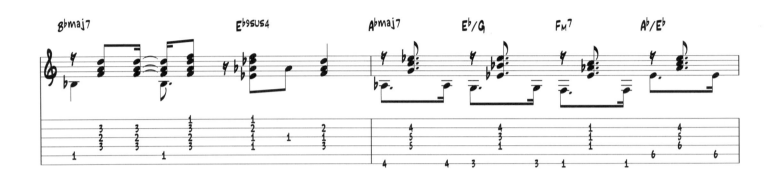
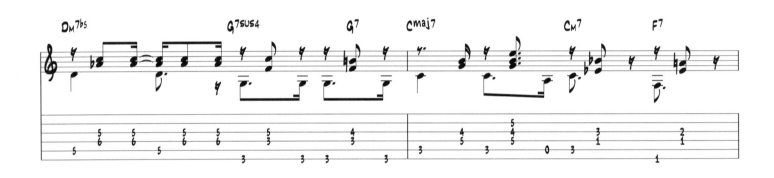
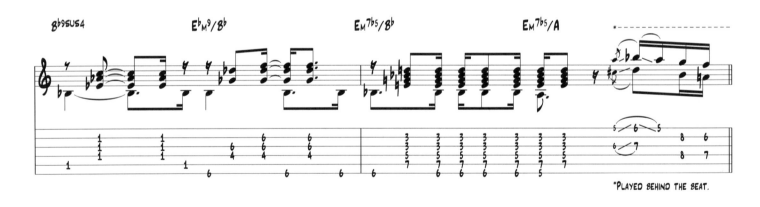

*PLAYED BEHIND THE BEAT.

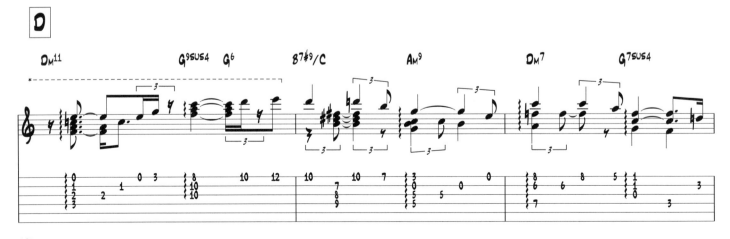

The Red One
By Pat Metheny

Medium Reggae ♩ = 100

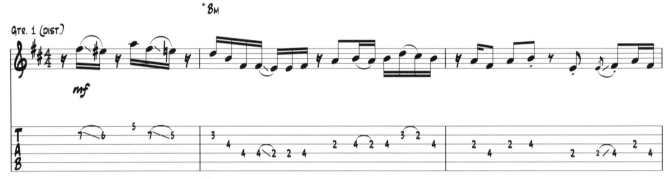

*Chord symbols reflect overall harmony.

Copyright © 1994, 2008 Pat Meth Music Corp.
All Rights Reserved   Used by Permission

*Sounds one octave higher than written. (Trumpet patch)

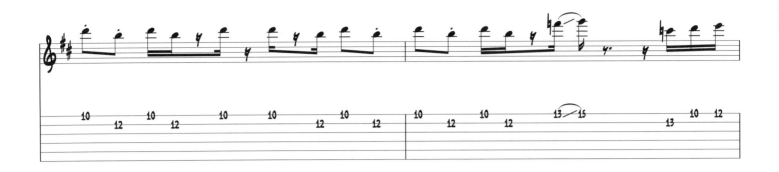
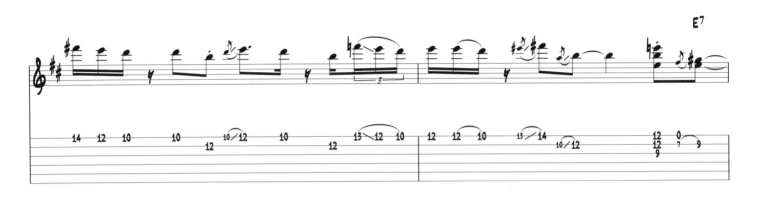

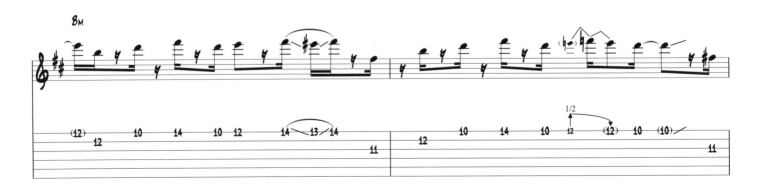

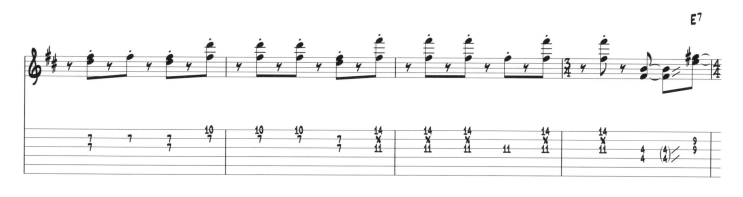

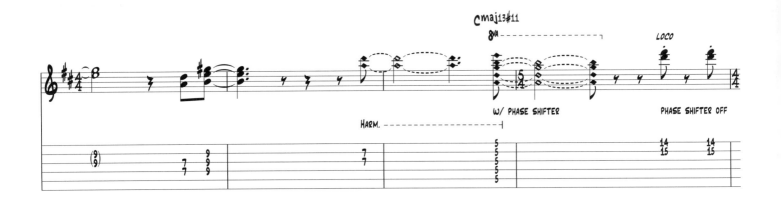
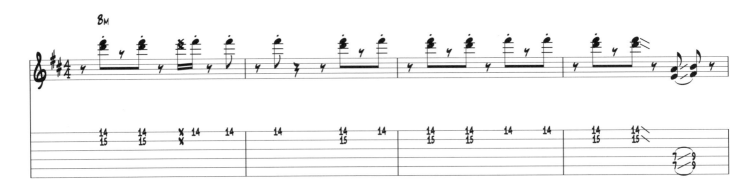
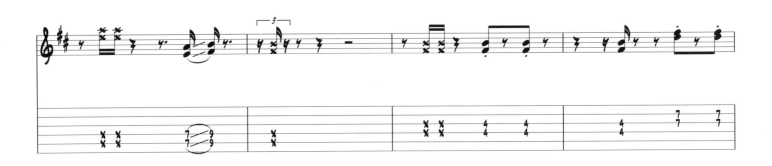
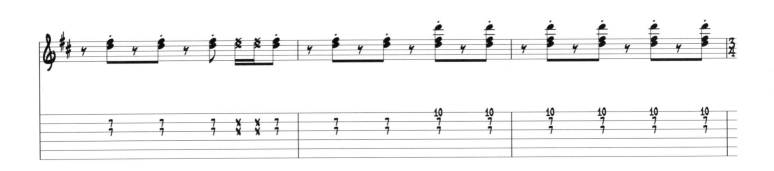
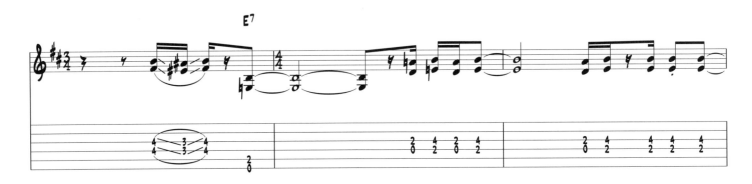

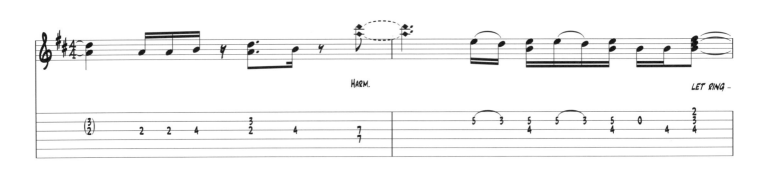

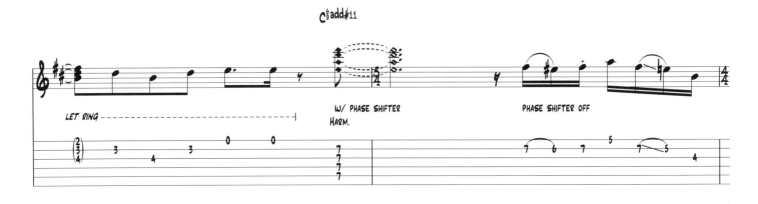

Day Trip
By Pat Metheny

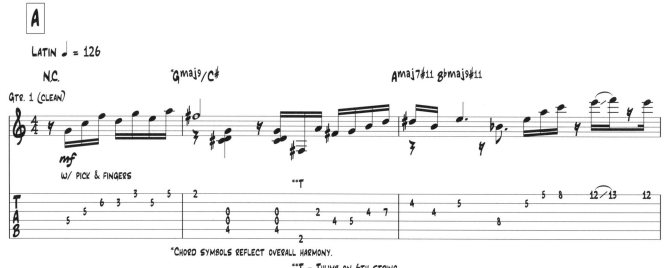
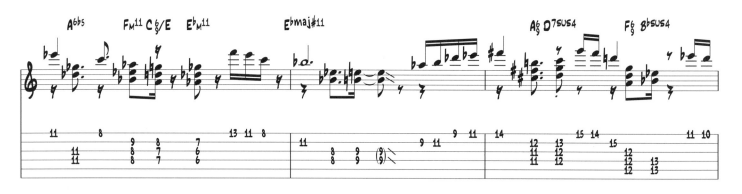

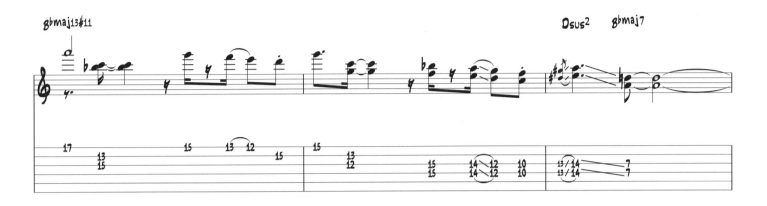
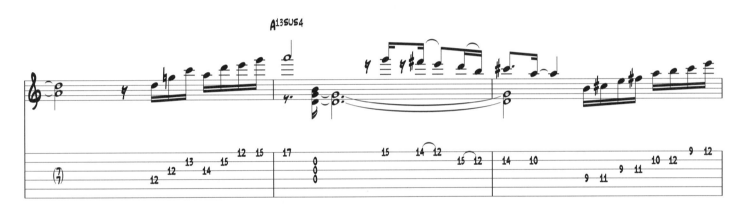
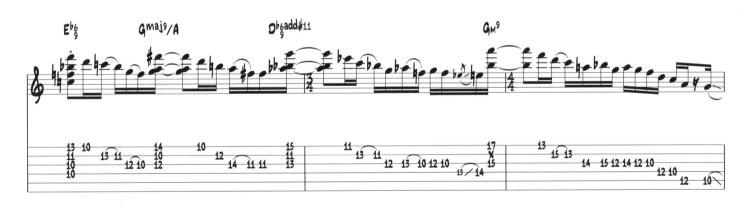

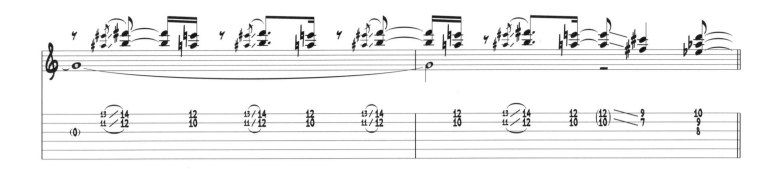

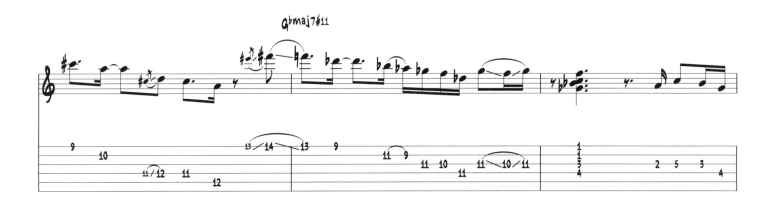

Abmaj7#11

Gmaj7#11   Gbmaj7

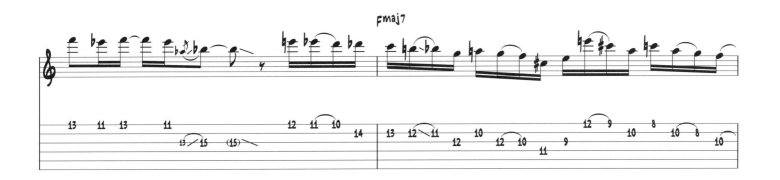
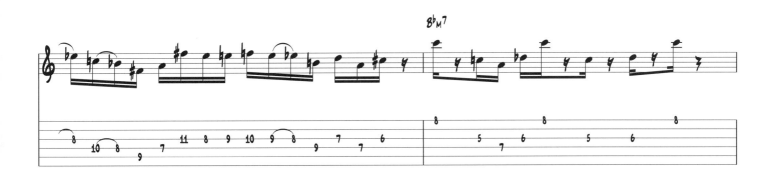
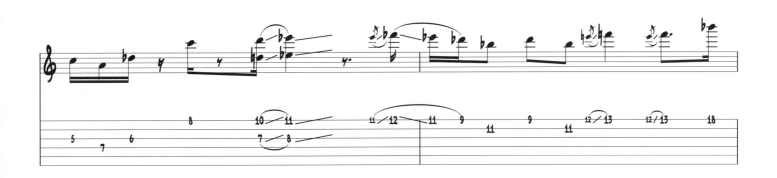
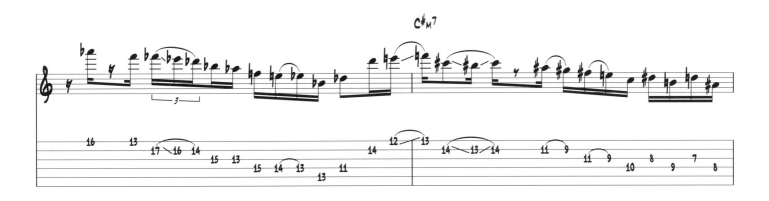

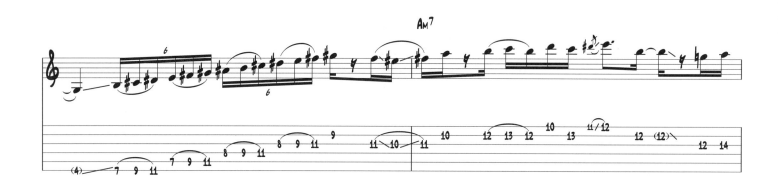

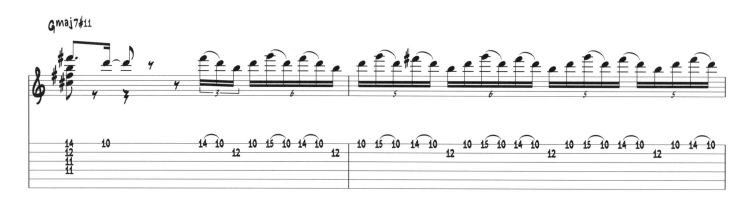

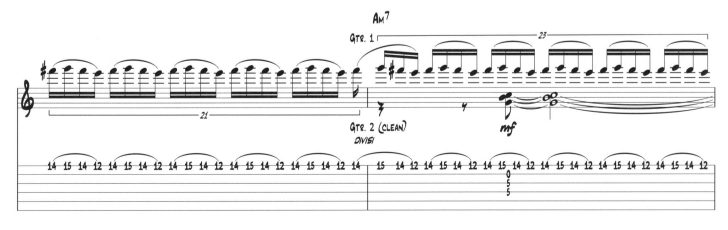

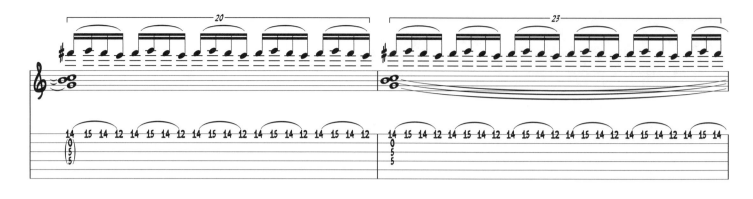

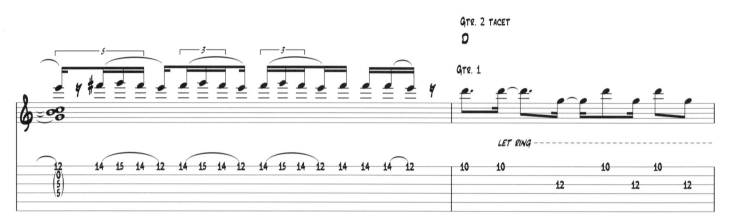

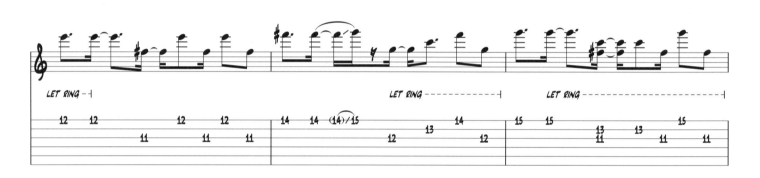

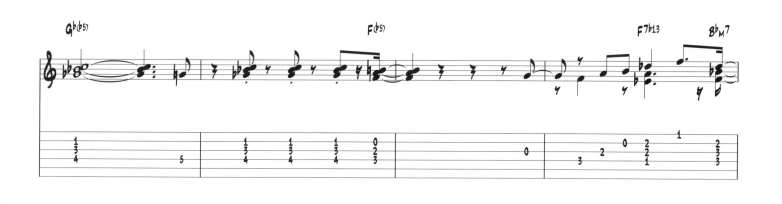

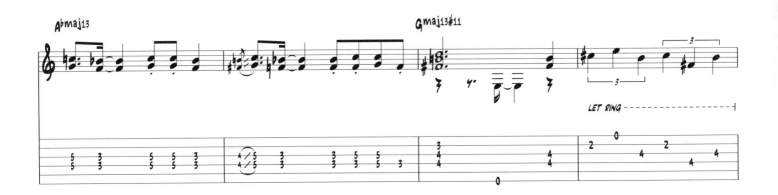

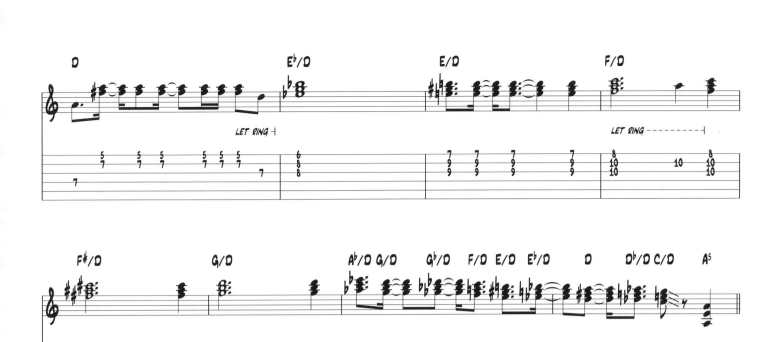

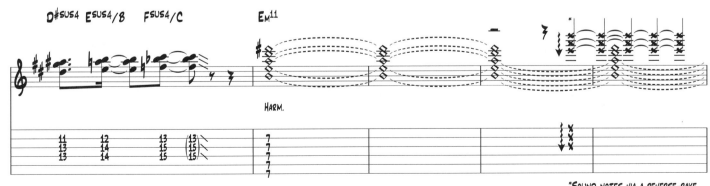

*Sound notes via a reverse-rake behind the nut.

134

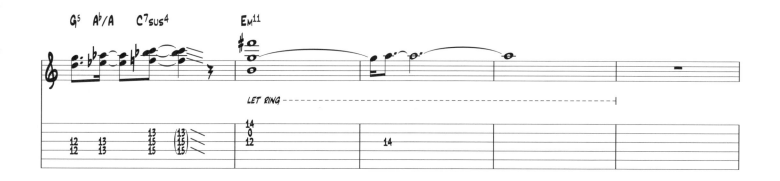
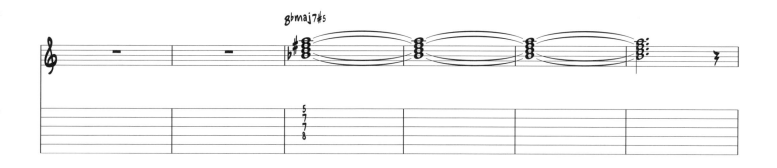

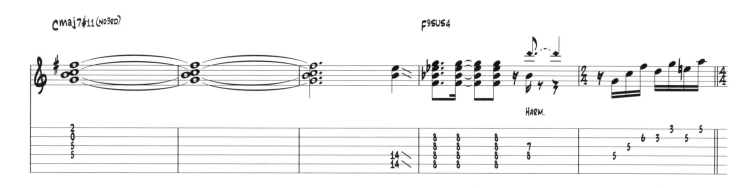

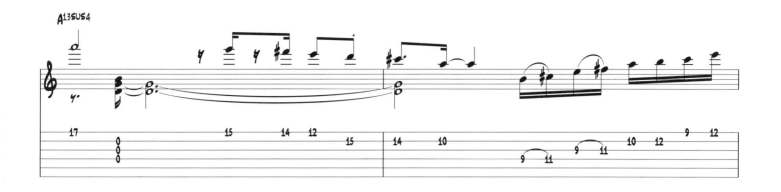
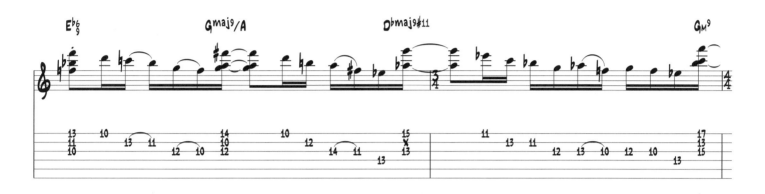
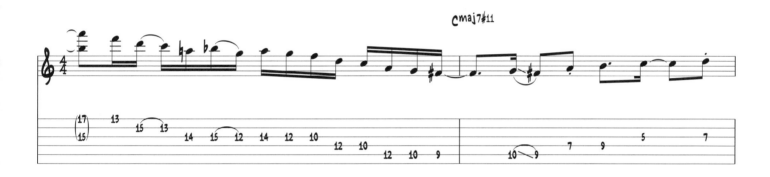
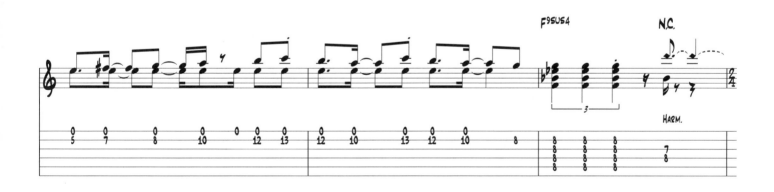

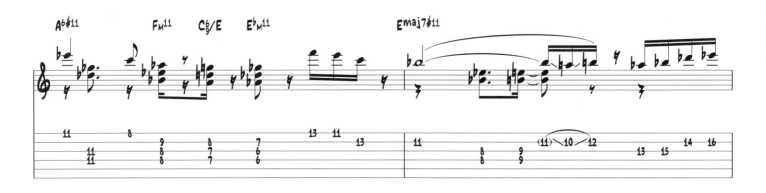

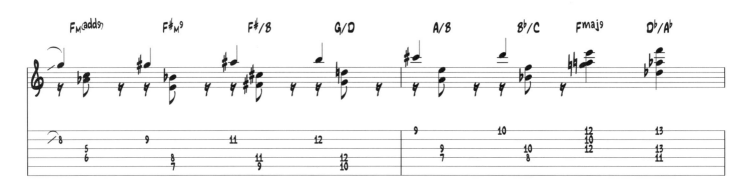
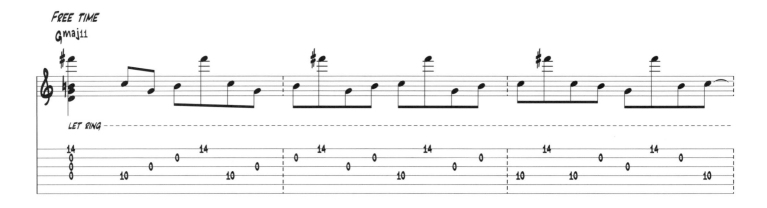
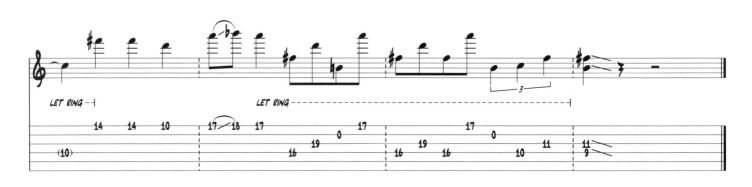

Tromsø
By Pat Metheny

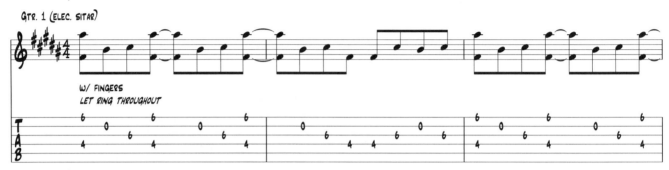
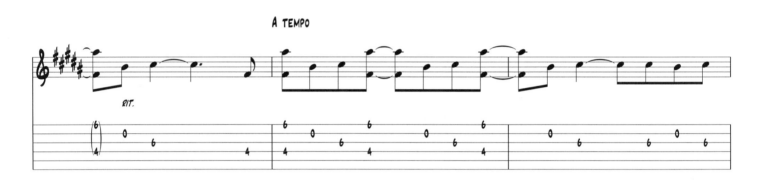
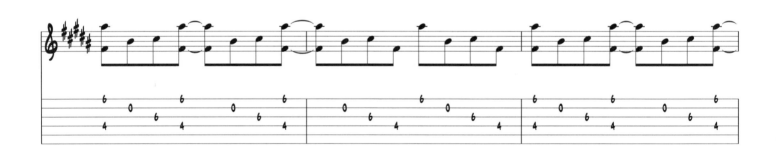
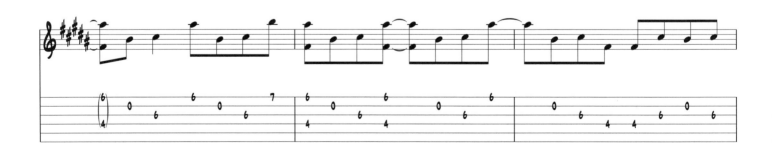

Copyright © 2008 Pat Meth Music Corp.
All Rights Reserved Used by Permission

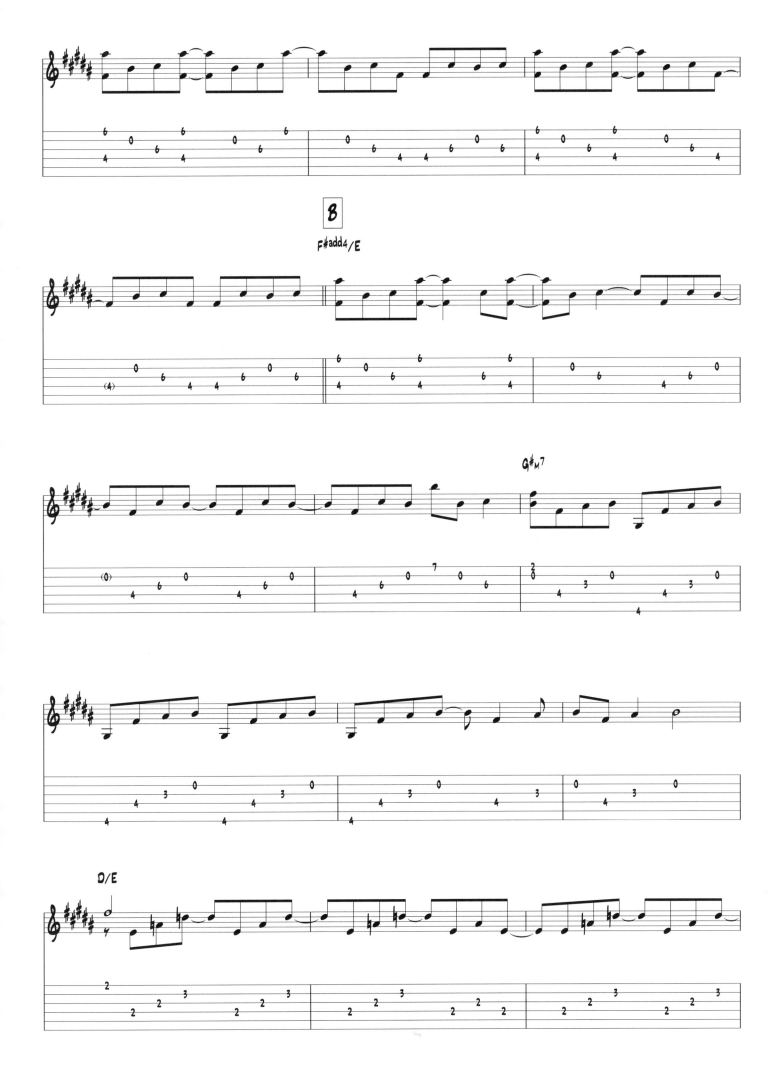

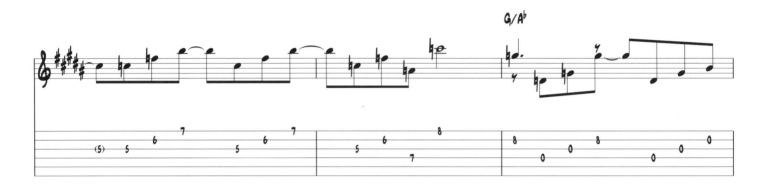

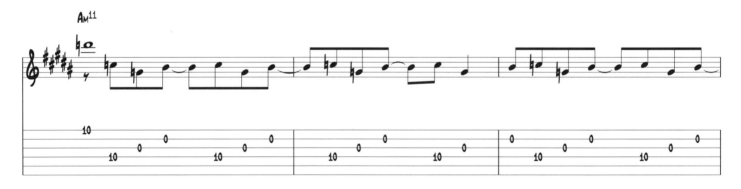

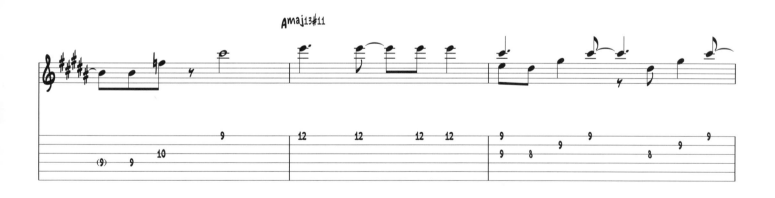

143

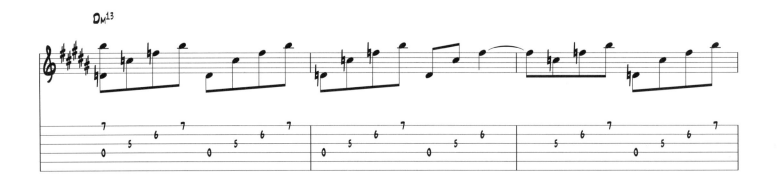

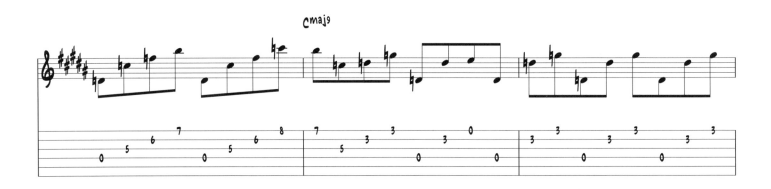

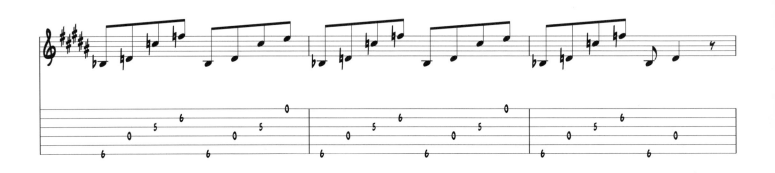

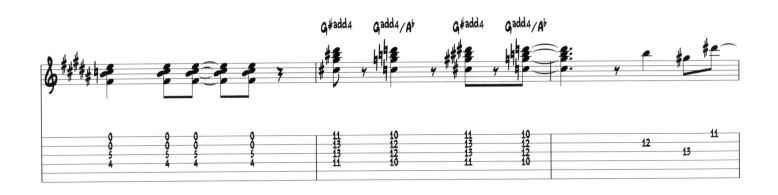

*Played behind the beat.

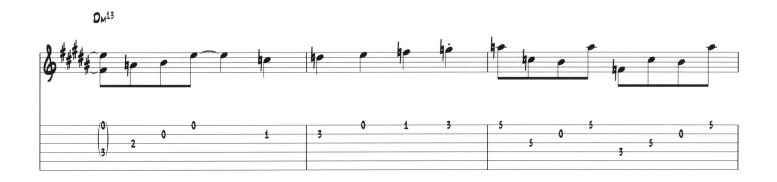

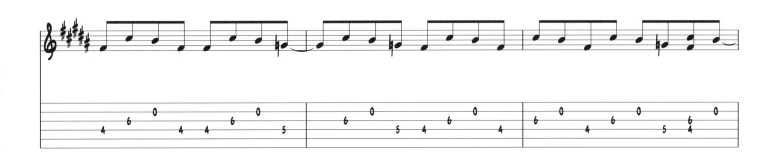

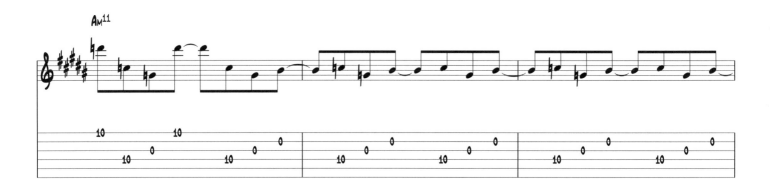

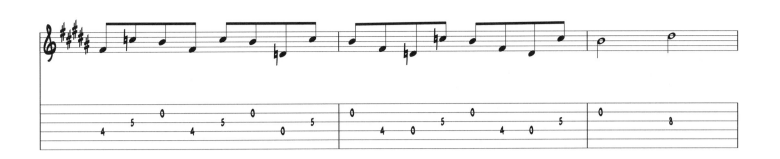
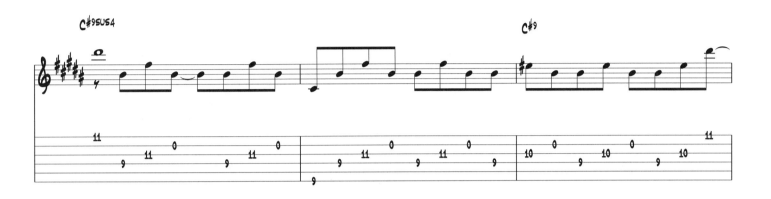

153

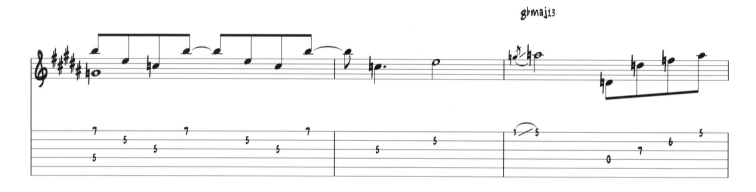
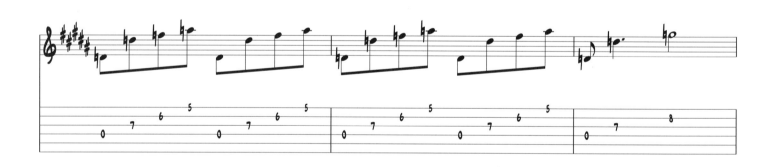
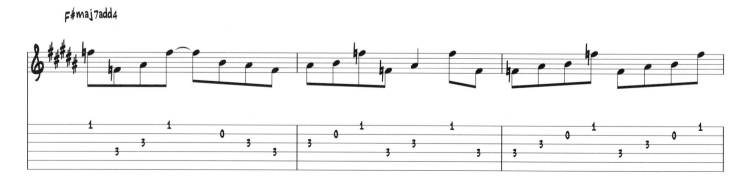

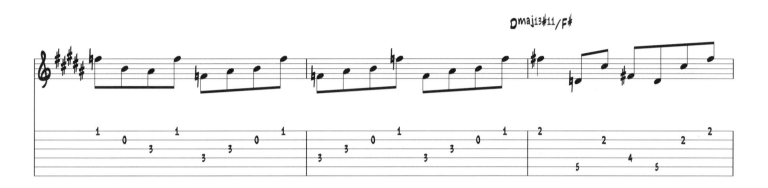

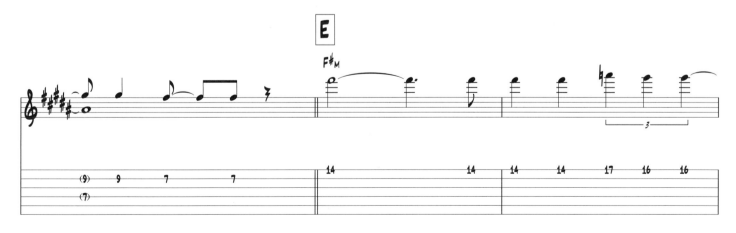

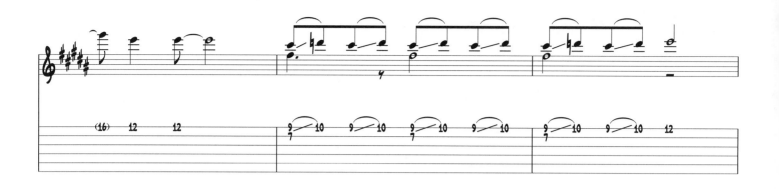

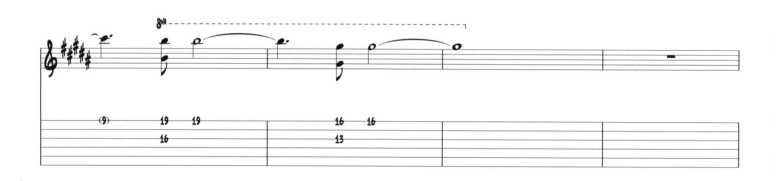
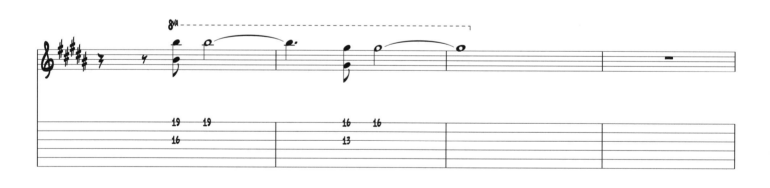
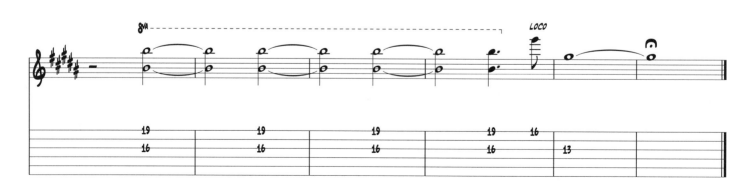

Traveling Fast
By Pat Metheny

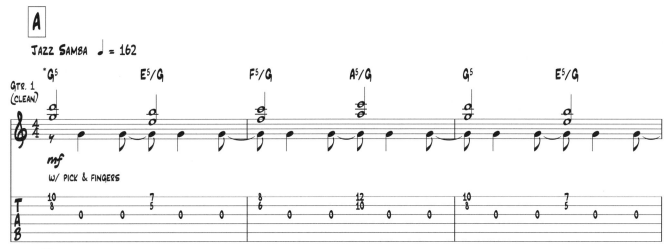

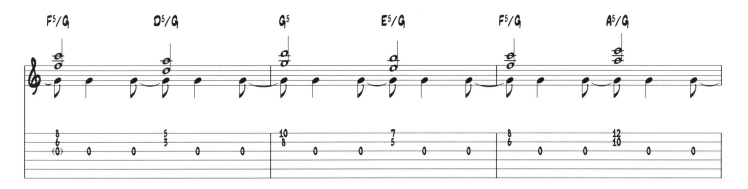

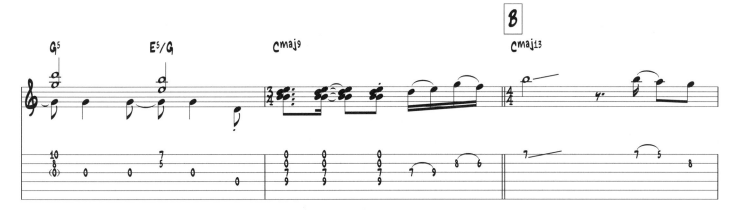

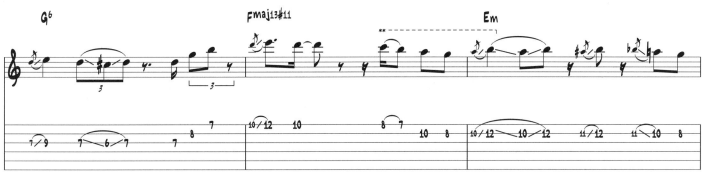

Copyright © 2008 Pat Meth Music Corp.
All Rights Reserved   Used by Permission

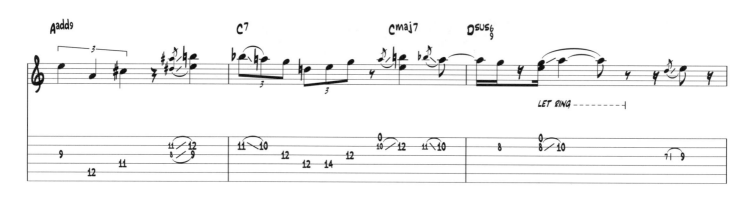
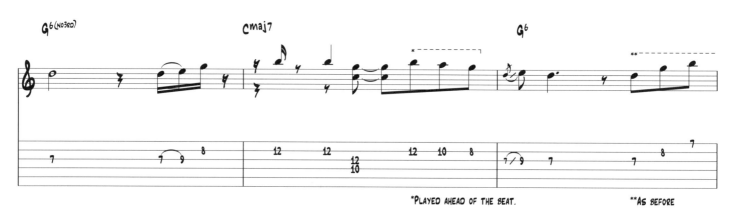

*Played ahead of the beat.   **As before

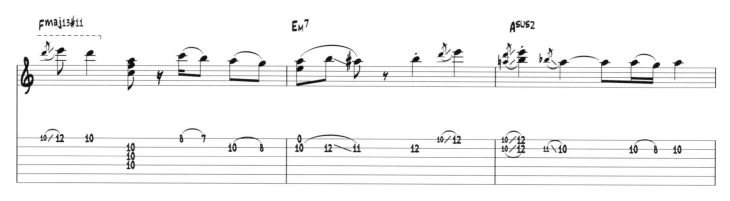
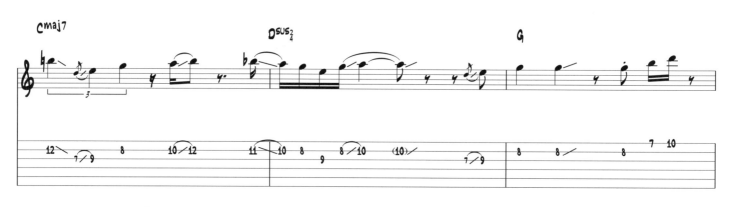

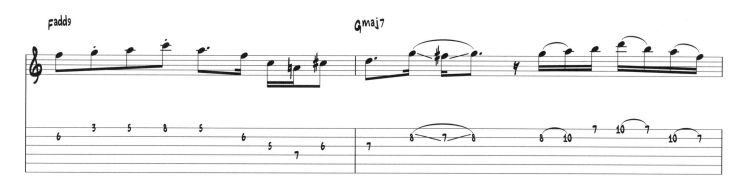

162

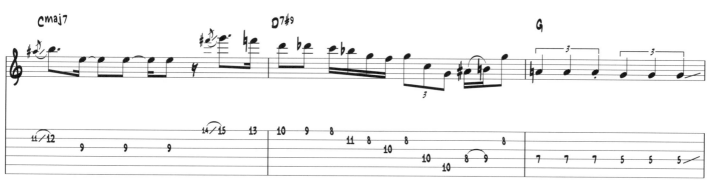

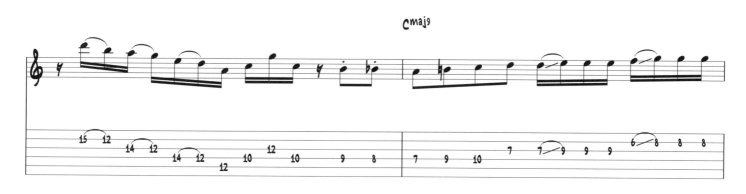

163

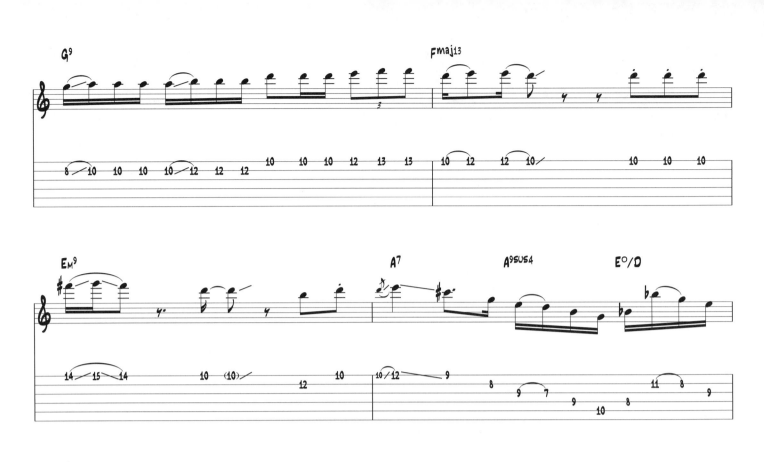
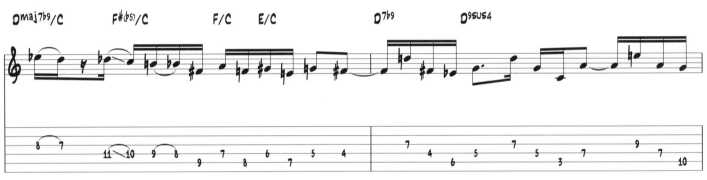
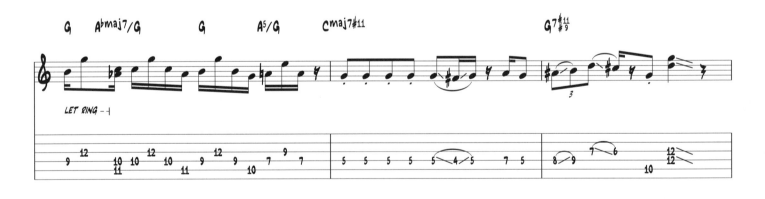
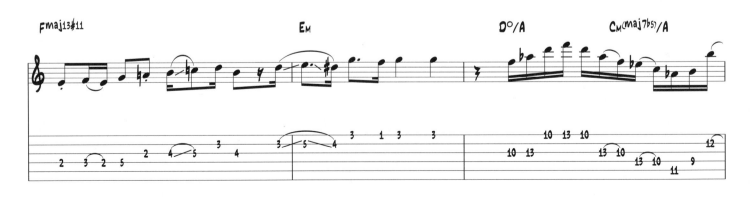

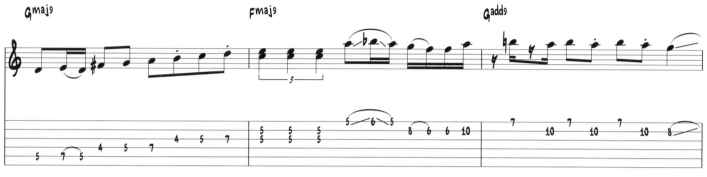

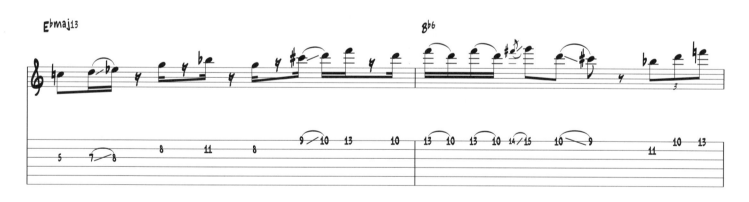
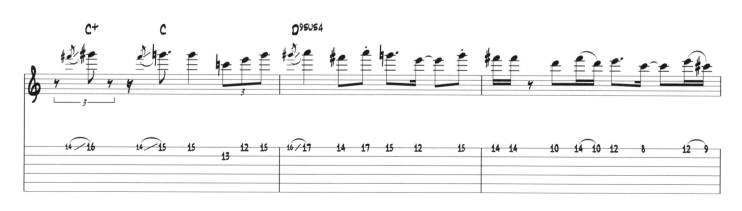

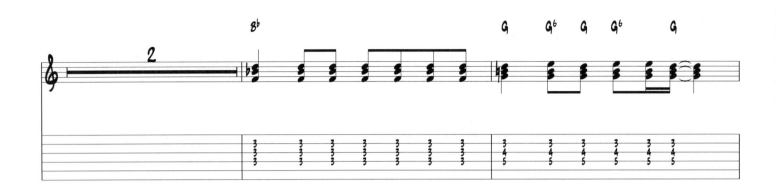

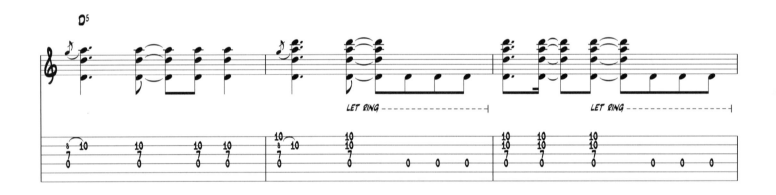

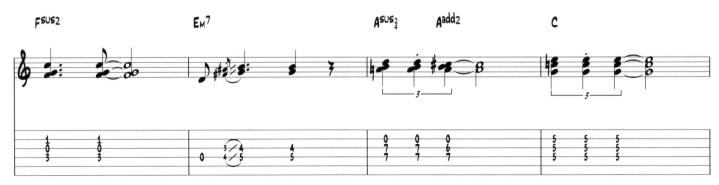

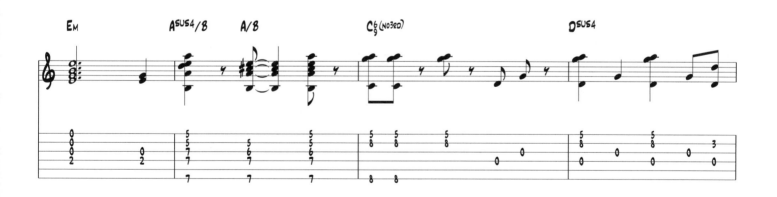
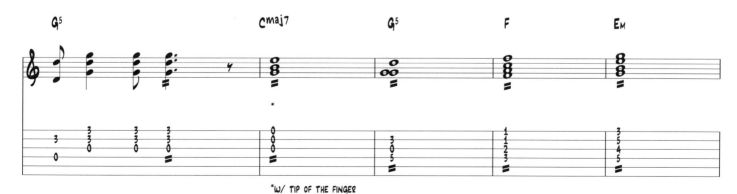

*w/ tip of the finger

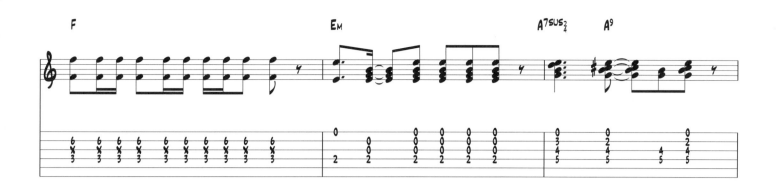
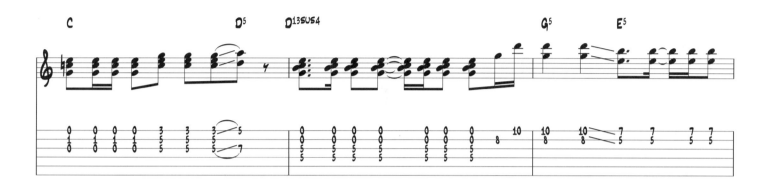
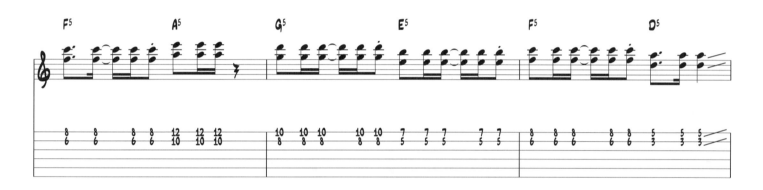

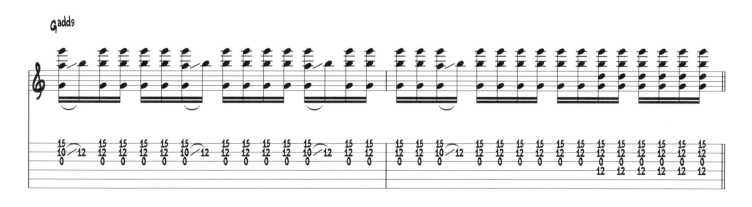

*Played ahead of the beat.

**Played behind the beat.

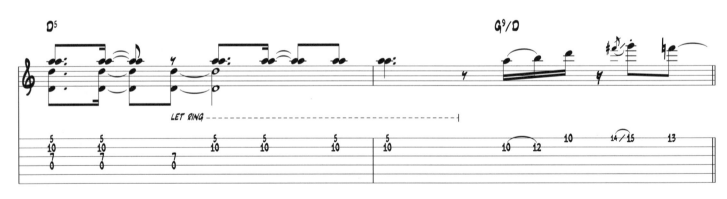
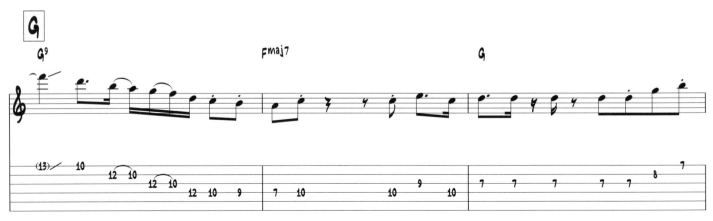

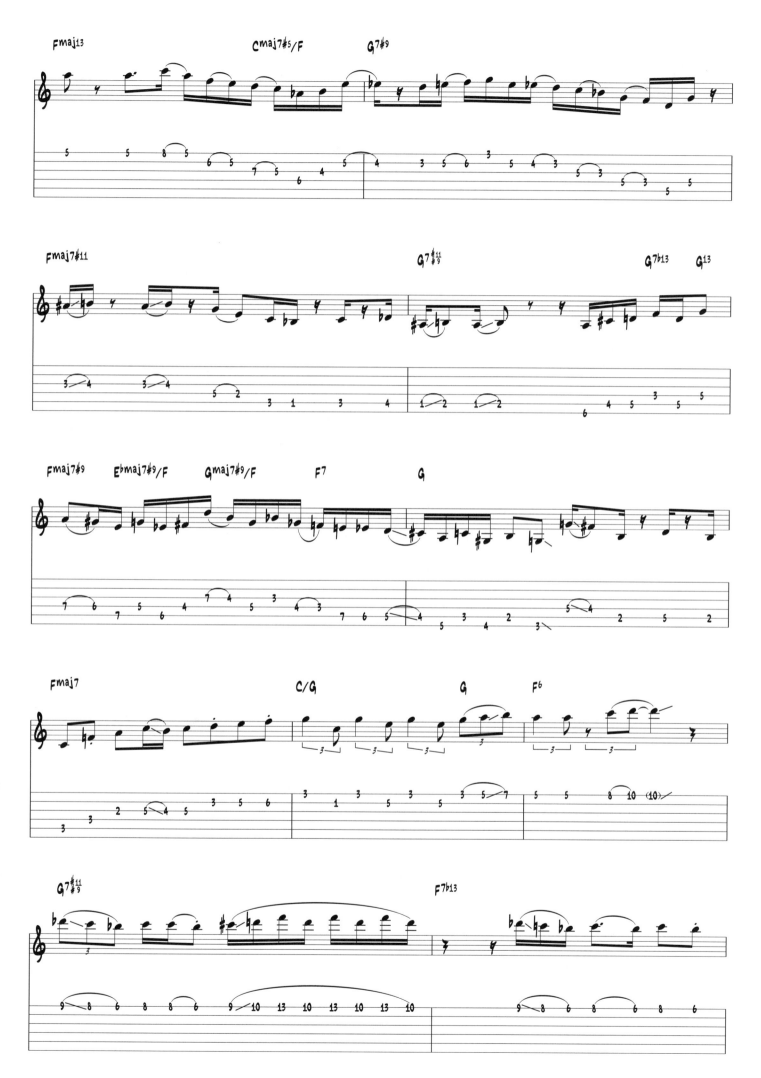

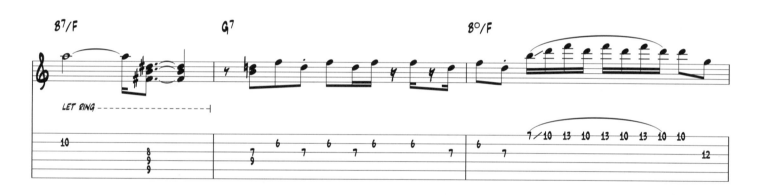
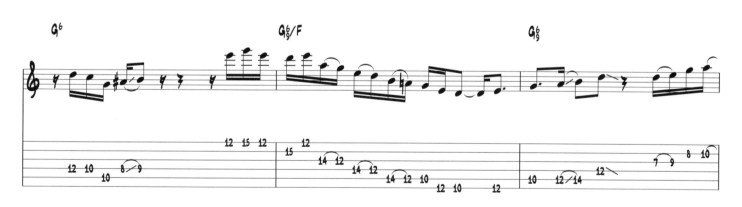

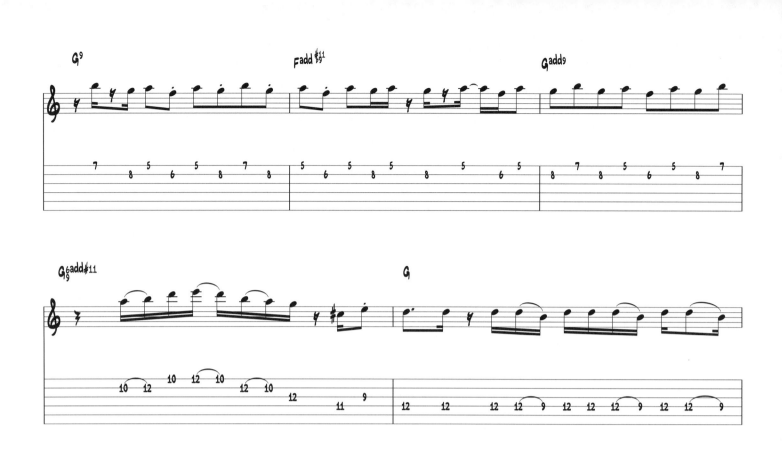
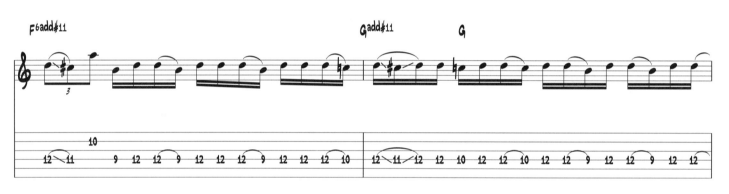
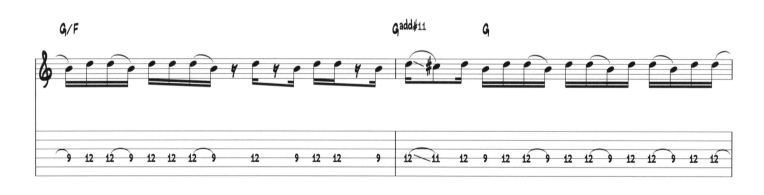
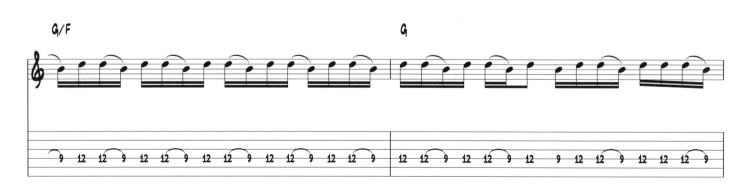

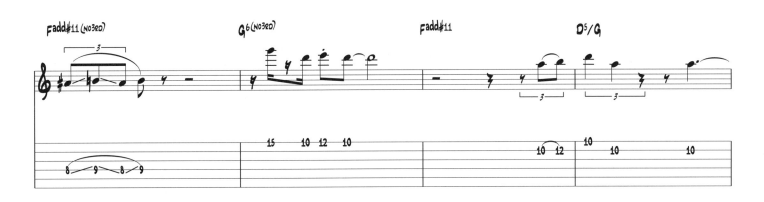
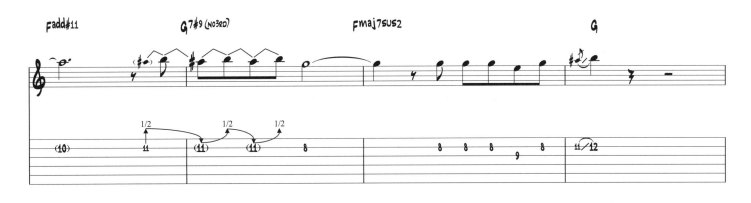
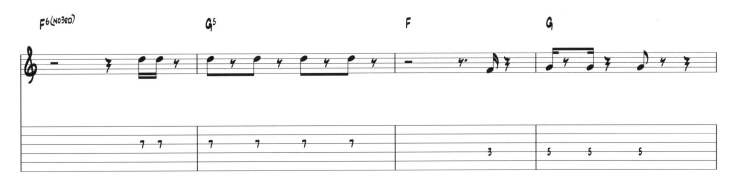

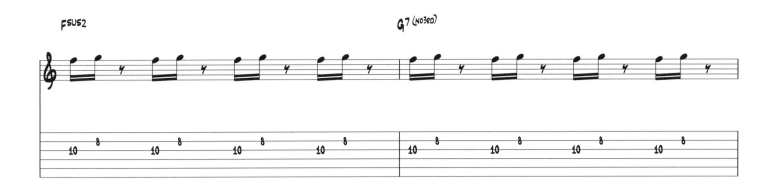
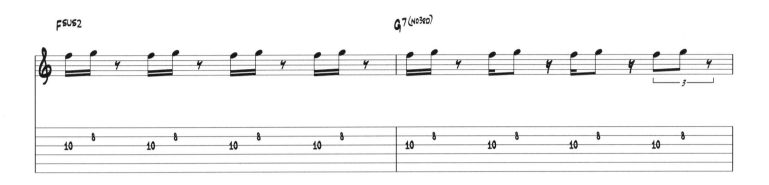
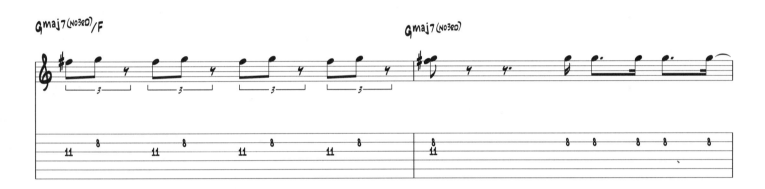
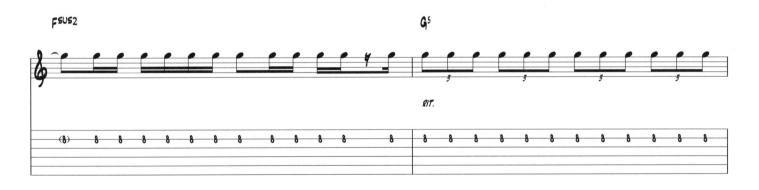
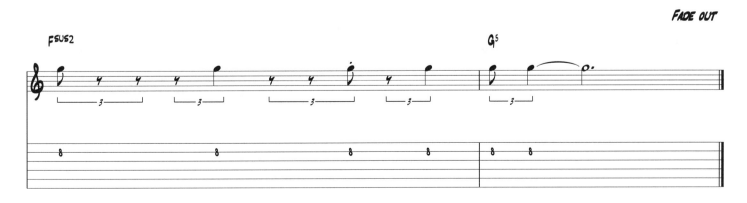

Inori

By Pat Metheny

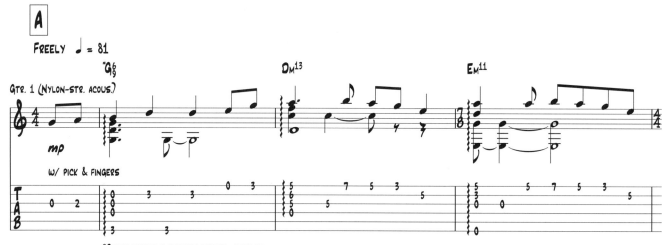
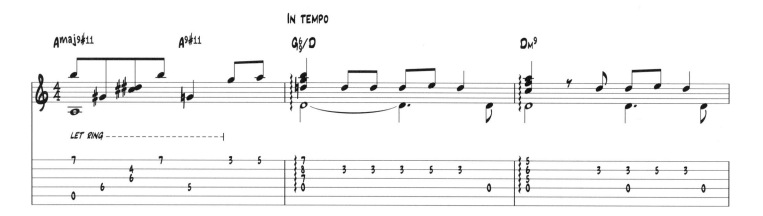
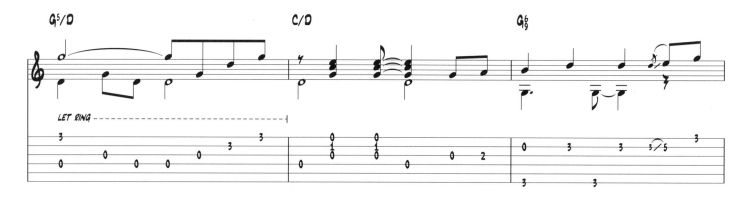

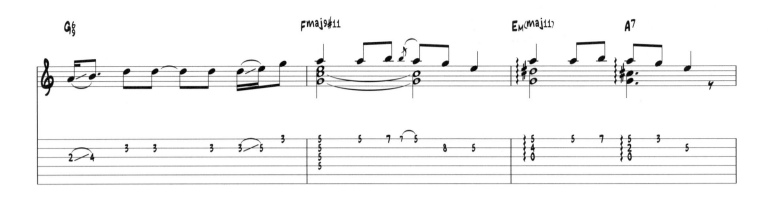

*Played behind the beat.

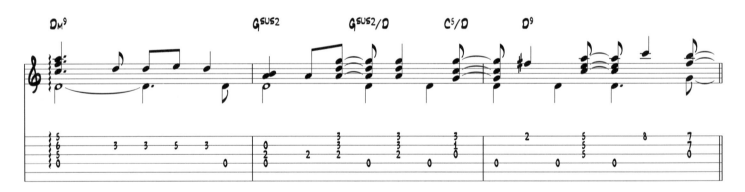
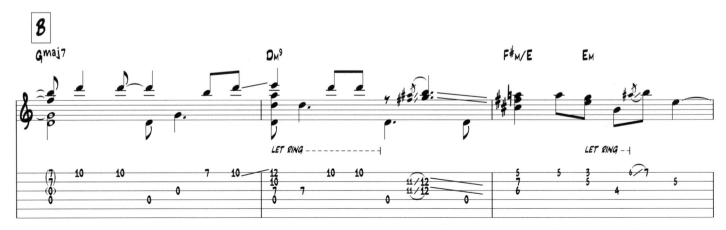

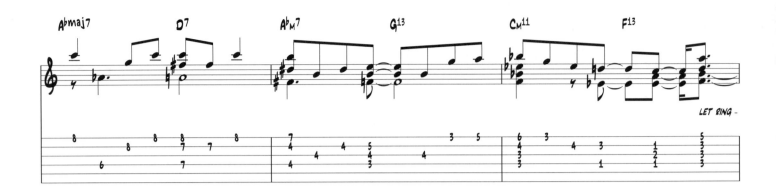
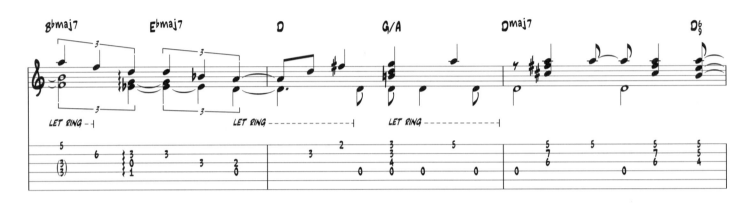

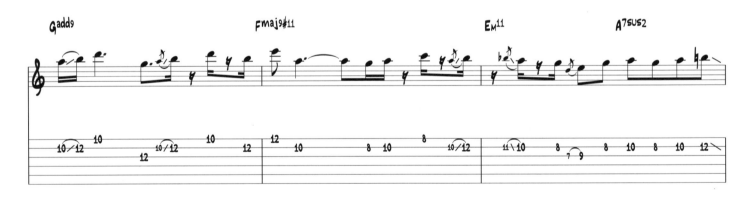
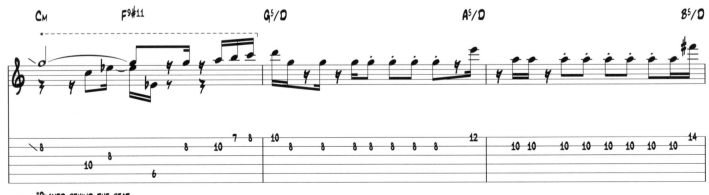

*Played behind the beat.

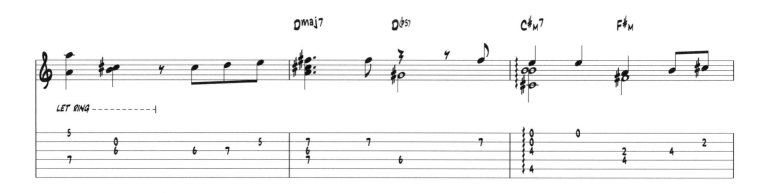

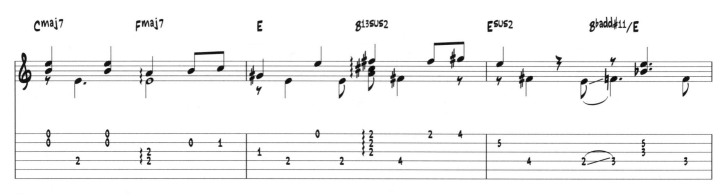

Back Arm & Blackcharge

By Pat Metheny

194

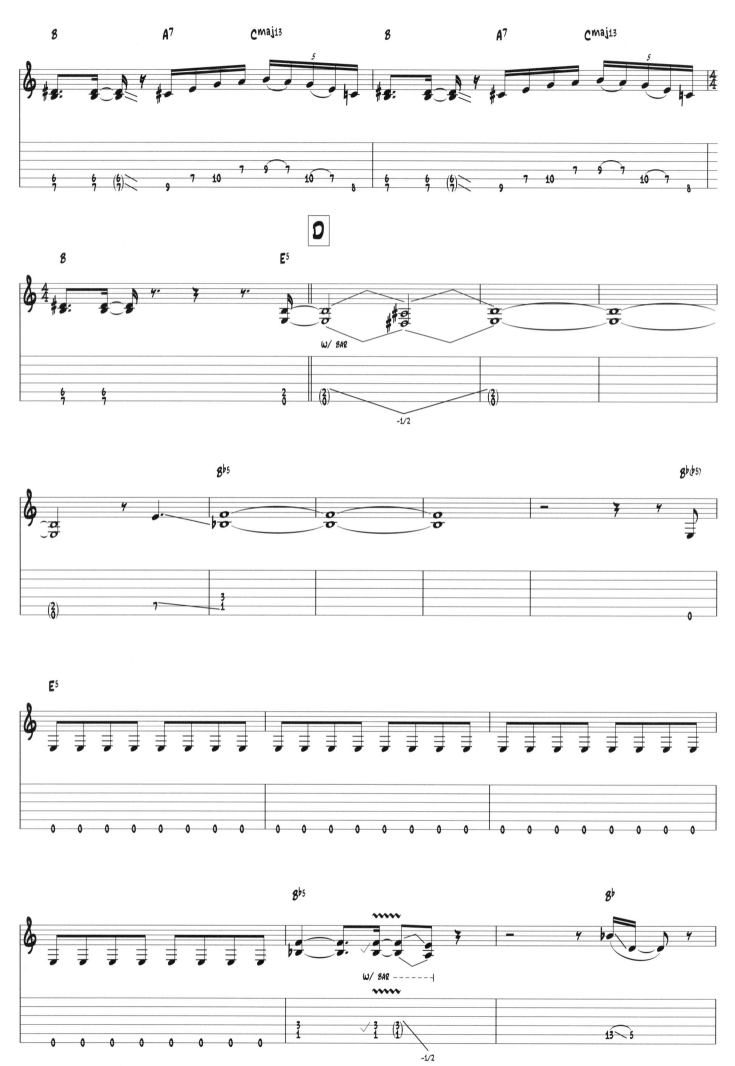

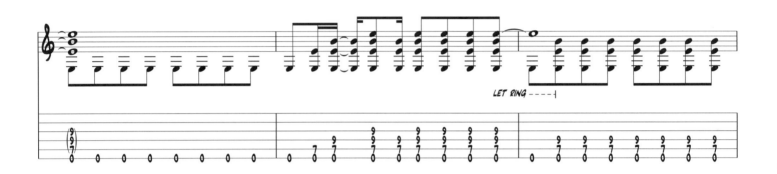
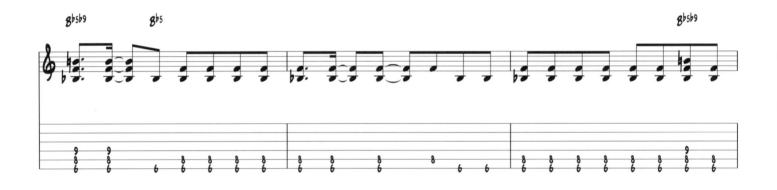
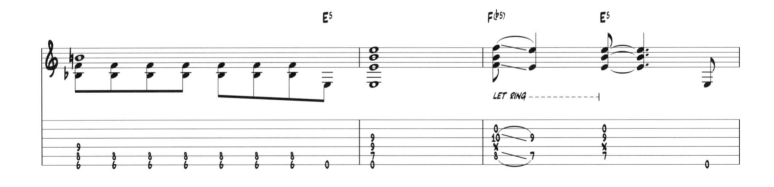

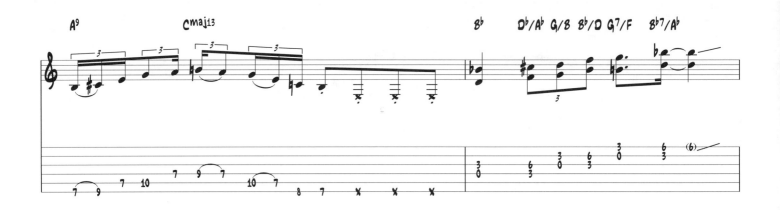

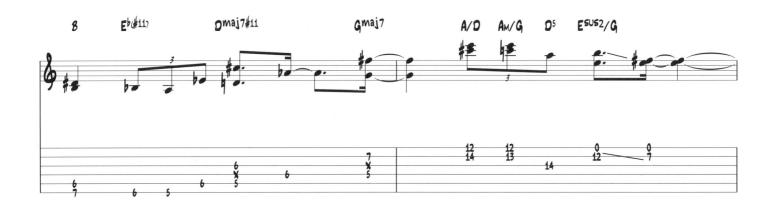

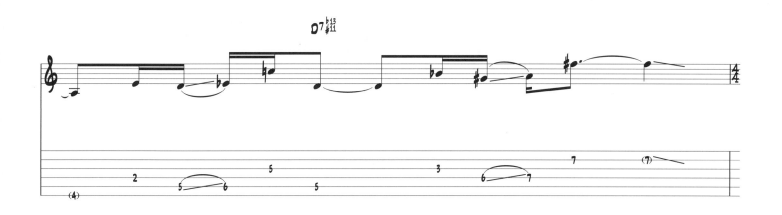
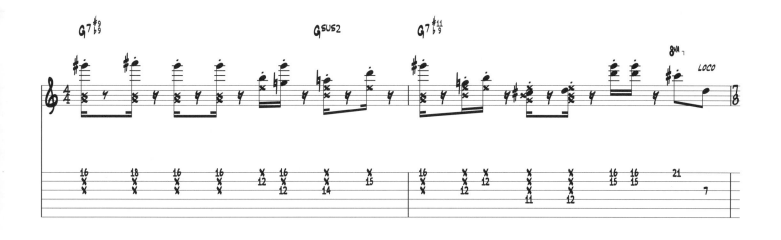

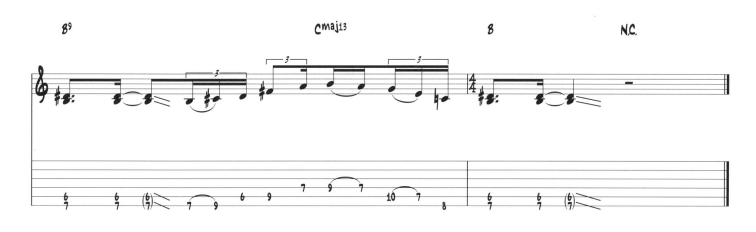

The Night Becomes You
By Pat Metheny

*Nashville tuning:
(low to high) A-D-G↑-C↑-E-A

*Replace middle two strings with thinner gauges to facilitate tuning them up one octave.
**Chord symbols reflect overall harmony. Notation and chord symbols have been written up a perfect 5th (relative to standard tuning) for ease of reading.

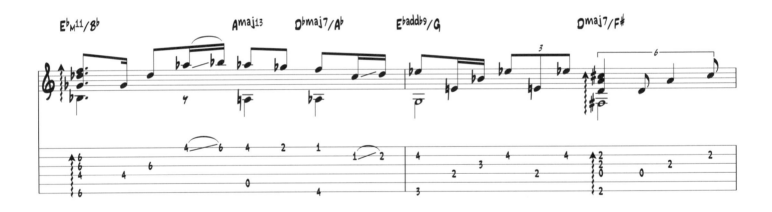

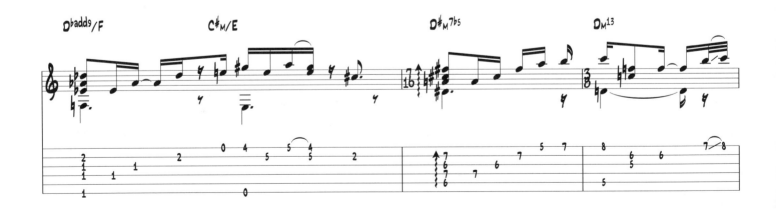

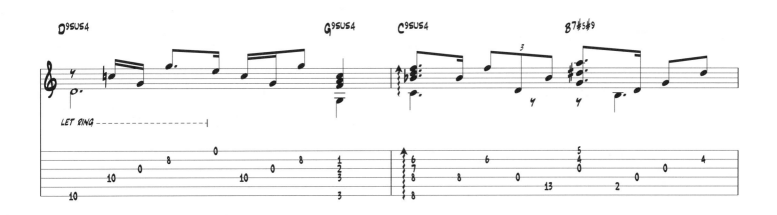

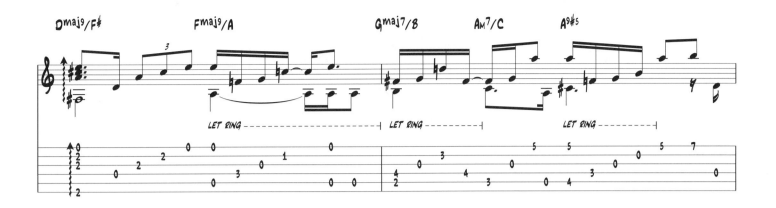
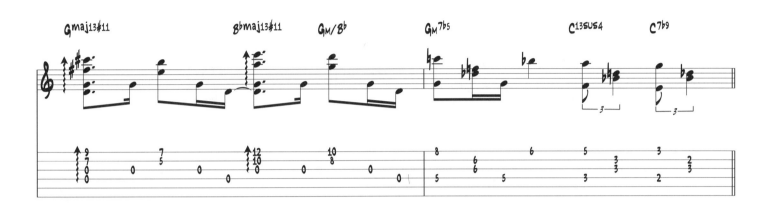

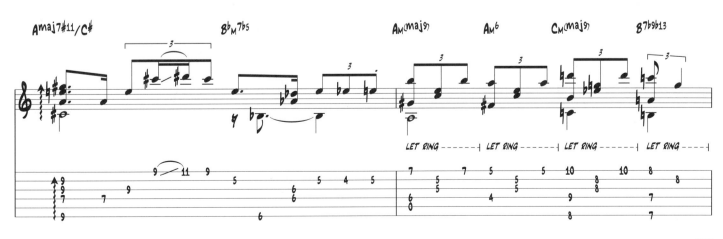

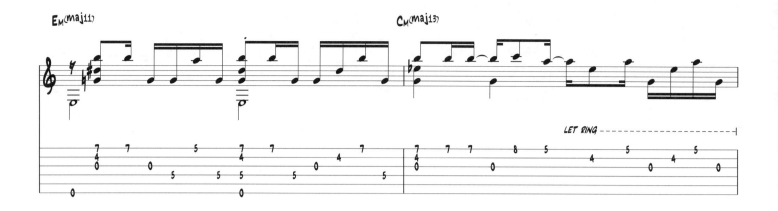

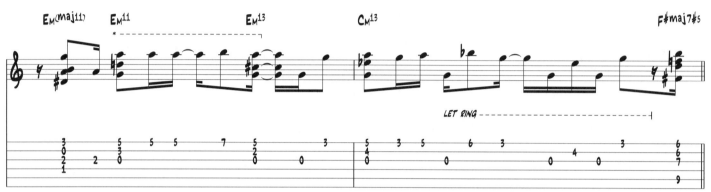

*Played behind the beat.

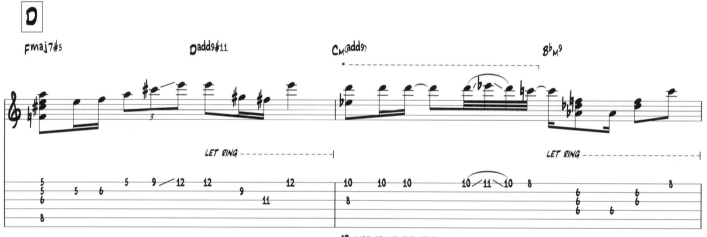

*Played behind the beat.

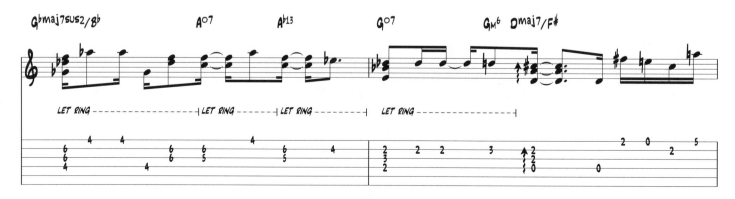

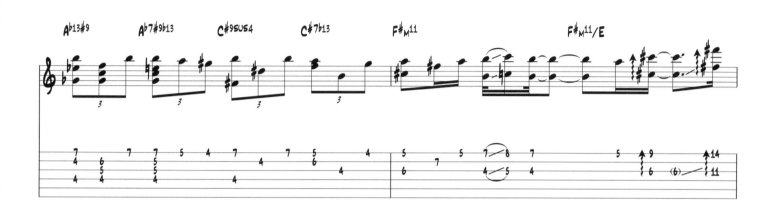
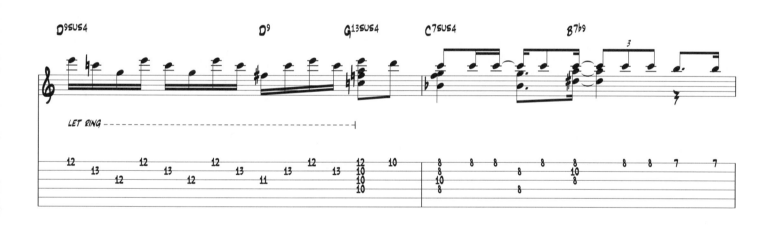

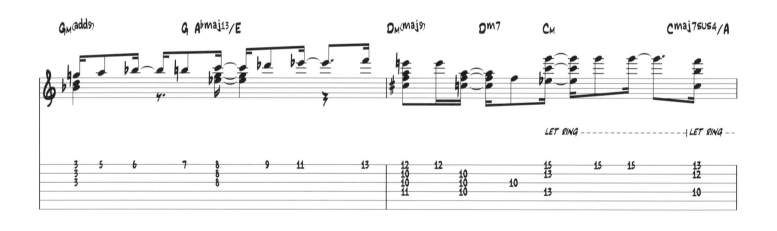
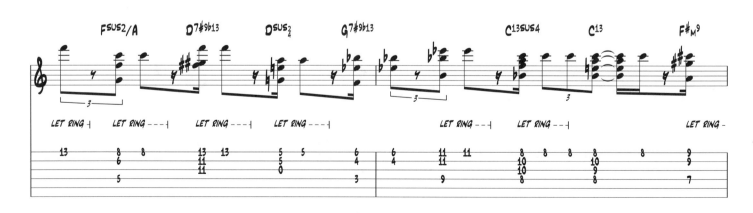

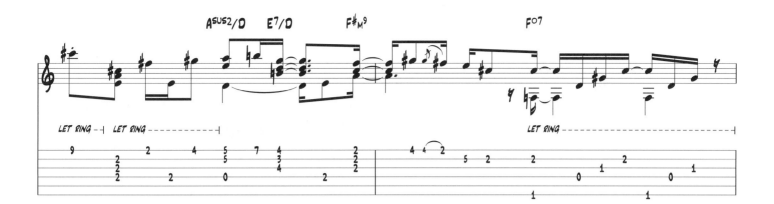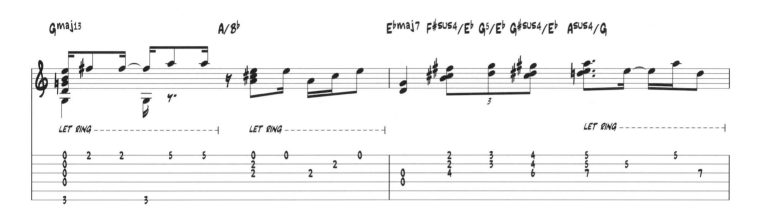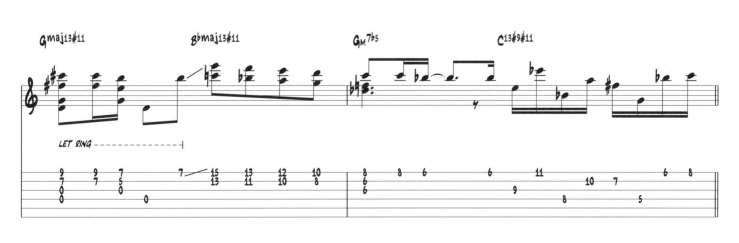

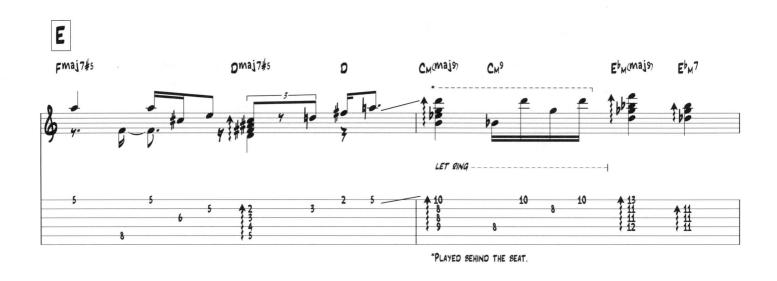
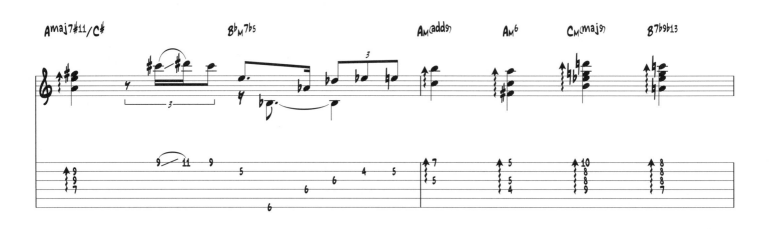
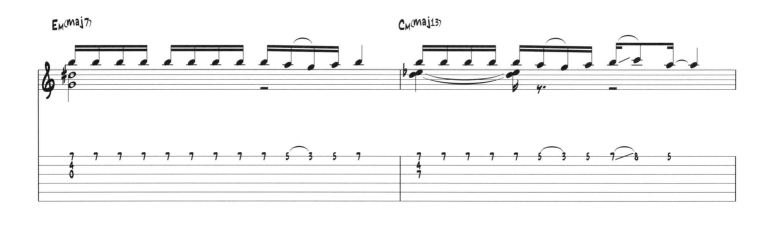
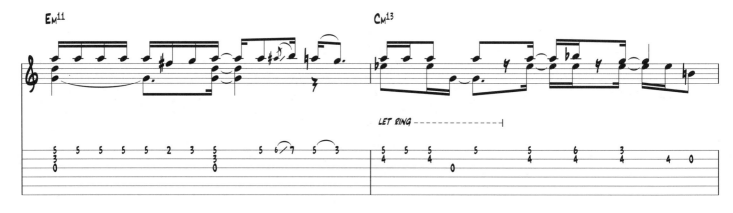

GUITAR NOTATION LEGEND

Guitar music can be notated three different ways: on a *musical staff*, in *tablature*, and in *rhythm slashes*.

RHYTHM SLASHES are written above the staff. Strum chords in the rhythm indicated. Use the chord diagrams found at the top of the first page of the transcription for the appropriate chord voicings. Round noteheads indicate single notes.

THE MUSICAL STAFF shows pitches and rhythms and is divided by bar lines into measures. Pitches are named after the first seven letters of the alphabet.

TABLATURE graphically represents the guitar fingerboard. Each horizontal line represents a string, and each number represents a fret.

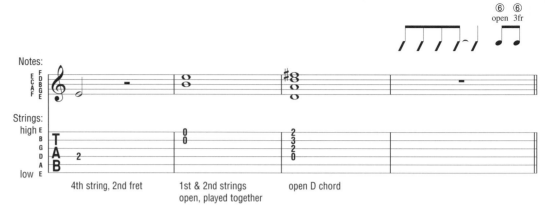

Definitions for Special Guitar Notation

HALF-STEP BEND: Strike the note and bend up 1/2 step.

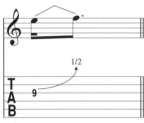

BEND AND RELEASE: Strike the note and bend up as indicated, then release back to the original note. Only the first note is struck.

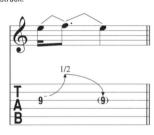

VIBRATO: The string is vibrated by rapidly bending and releasing the note with the fretting hand.

LEGATO SLIDE: Strike the first note and then slide the same fret-hand finger up or down to the second note. The second note is not struck.

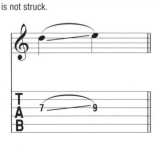

WHOLE-STEP BEND: Strike the note and bend up one step.

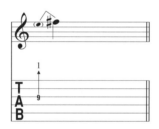

PRE-BEND: Bend the note as indicated, then strike it.

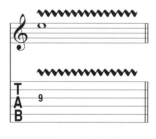

WIDE VIBRATO: The pitch is varied to a greater degree by vibrating with the fretting hand.

SHIFT SLIDE: Same as legato slide, except the second note is struck.

GRACE NOTE BEND: Strike the note and immediately bend up as indicated.

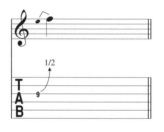

PRE-BEND AND RELEASE: Bend the note as indicated. Strike it and release the bend back to the original note.

HAMMER-ON: Strike the first (lower) note with one finger, then sound the higher note (on the same string) with another finger by fretting it without picking.

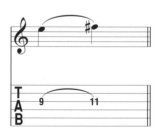

TRILL: Very rapidly alternate between the notes indicated by continuously hammering on and pulling off.

SLIGHT (MICROTONE) BEND: Strike the note and bend up 1/4 step.

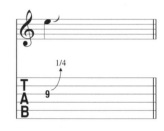

UNISON BEND: Strike the two notes simultaneously and bend the lower note up to the pitch of the higher.

PULL-OFF: Place both fingers on the notes to be sounded. Strike the first note and without picking, pull the finger off to sound the second (lower) note.

TAPPING: Hammer ("tap") the fret indicated with the pick-hand index or middle finger and pull off to the note fretted by the fret hand.

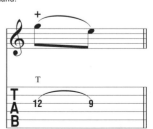

NATURAL HARMONIC: Strike the note while the fret-hand lightly touches the string directly over the fret indicated.

PINCH HARMONIC: The note is fretted normally and a harmonic is produced by adding the edge of the thumb or the tip of the index finger of the pick hand to the normal pick attack.

HARP HARMONIC: The note is fretted normally and a harmonic is produced by gently resting the pick hand's index finger directly above the indicated fret (in parentheses) while the pick hand's thumb or pick assists by plucking the appropriate string.

PICK SCRAPE: The edge of the pick is rubbed down (or up) the string, producing a scratchy sound.

 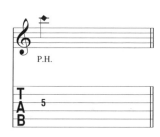 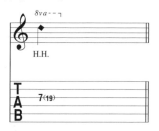 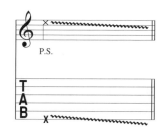

MUFFLED STRINGS: A percussive sound is produced by laying the fret hand across the string(s) without depressing, and striking them with the pick hand.

PALM MUTING: The note is partially muted by the pick hand lightly touching the string(s) just before the bridge.

RAKE: Drag the pick across the strings indicated with a single motion.

TREMOLO PICKING: The note is picked as rapidly and continuously as possible.

 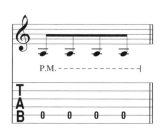 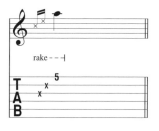 

ARPEGGIATE: Play the notes of the chord indicated by quickly rolling them from bottom to top.

VIBRATO BAR DIVE AND RETURN: The pitch of the note or chord is dropped a specified number of steps (in rhythm), then returned to the original pitch.

VIBRATO BAR SCOOP: Depress the bar just before striking the note, then quickly release the bar.

VIBRATO BAR DIP: Strike the note and then immediately drop a specified number of steps, then release back to the original pitch.

 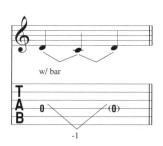  

Additional Musical Definitions

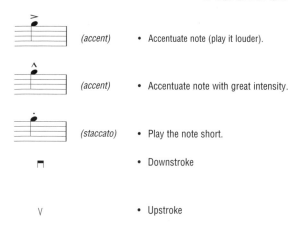

(accent)	• Accentuate note (play it louder).	**Rhy. Fig.**	• Label used to recall a recurring accompaniment pattern (usually chordal).
(accent)	• Accentuate note with great intensity.	**Riff**	• Label used to recall composed, melodic lines (usually single notes) which recur.
(staccato)	• Play the note short.	**Fill**	• Label used to identify a brief melodic figure which is to be inserted into the arrangement.
	• Downstroke	**Rhy. Fill**	• A chordal version of a Fill.
V	• Upstroke	tacet	• Instrument is silent (drops out).
D.S. al Coda	• Go back to the sign (𝄋), then play until the measure marked "***To Coda***," then skip to the section labelled "***Coda***."		• Repeat measures between signs.
D.C. al Fine	• Go back to the beginning of the song and play until the measure marked "***Fine***" (end).		• When a repeated section has different endings, play the first ending only the first time and the second ending only the second time.

NOTE: Tablature numbers in parentheses mean:
    1. The note is being sustained over a system (note in standard notation is tied), or
    2. The note is sustained, but a new articulation (such as a hammer-on, pull-off, slide or vibrato) begins, or
    3. The note is a barely audible "ghost" note (note in standard notation is also in parentheses).

OUTSTANDING PAT METHENY COLLECTIONS

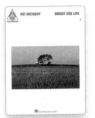

PAT METHENY – BRIGHT SIZE LIFE
INCLUDES TAB
Note-for-note guitar transcriptions (carefully reviewed and approved by Metheny himself!) for all 8 songs from his highly acclaimed 1975 studio debut – which also features one of the earliest recordings of bass legend Jaco Pastorius. Includes: Bright Size Life • Midwestern Nights Dream • Missouri Uncompromised • Omaha Celebration • Round Trip/Broadway Blues • Sirabhorn • Uniquity Road • Unity Village. Contains jazz-style handwritten notation and tablature, a full-page photo of Metheny, and a Guitar Notation Legend.

00690562   Guitar Recorded Versions..................... $19.95

PAT METHENY – DAY TRIP/TOKYO DAY TRIP
INCLUDES TAB
Transcriptions to all the tracks from Metheny's 2008 one-day-long recording session with bassist Christian McBride and drummer Antonio Sanchez, plus five tracks recorded live in Tokyo, including: At Last You're Here • Black Arm & Black Charge • Calvin's Keys • Day Trip • Dreaming Trees • Inori • Is This America? • Let's Move • The Night Becomes You • The Red One • Snova • Son of Thirteen • Traveling Fast • Troms0 • When We Were Free.

00691073   Guitar Recorded Versions $22.99

PAT METHENY GUITAR WARM-UPS
Ever wonder how jazz guitar great Pat Metheny could be so creative and unpredictable? Take a lesson from your hero with these original warm-ups from the man himself. This collection of 14 guitar etudes will help you to limber up, improve picking technique, and build finger independence.

00696587 .... $14.99

PAT METHENY – ONE QUIET NIGHT
INCLUDES TAB
All 12 songs from the 2003 acoustic guitar recording by Metheny: Another Chance • Don't Know Why • Ferry 'Cross the Mersey • I Will Find the Way • Last Train Home • My Song • North to South, East to West • One Quiet Night • Over on 4th Street • Peace Memory • Song for the Boys • Time Goes On.

00690646   Guitar Recorded Versions $19.95

PAT METHENY – ORCHESTRION
THE COMPLETE SCORE
Metheny says, "'Orchestrionics' is the term that I am using to describe a method of developing ensemble-oriented music using acoustic and acoustoelectric musical instruments that are mechanically controlled in a variety of ways ... with the pieces on this particular recording leaning toward the compositional side of the spectrum. On top of these layers of acoustic sound, I add my conventional electric guitar playing as an improvised component." Here are the original scores for the five compositions: Entry Point • Expansion • Orchestrion • Soul Search • Spirit of the Air.

00001339   Scores..................................... $19.99

PAT METHENY – QUESTION AND ANSWER
INCLUDES TAB
Note-for-note transcriptions with tab, in a handwritten jazz-style font and supervised by Metheny himself. Includes all the songs from this 1989 album that the All Music Guide describes as "nine tracks of sheer jazz joy," calling Pat's playing "modernistic, highly fluid, almost liquid lightning." Songs: All the Things You Are • Change of Heart • H & H • Law Years • Never Too Far Away • Old Folks • Question & Answer • Solar • Three Flights Up.

00690559   Guitar Recorded Versions $19.95

PAT METHENY – REJOICING
INCLUDES TAB
Matching folio to the 1983 recording which *The All Music Guide* calls "an excellent set of memorable and unpredictable music." Includes 8 songs: Blues for Pat • The Calling • Humpty Dumpty • Lonely Woman • Rejoicing • Story from a Stranger • Tears Inside • Waiting for an Answer.

00690565   Guitar Recorded Versions . . . $19.95

PAT METHENY SONGBOOK
This amazing book is a complete collection of lead sheets for every song this revered and prolific guitarist/composer has ever written. This comprehensive tribute features: a two-page time line of Pat Metheny milestones; a biography; a complete full-color discography including album covers, musician credits and commentary from Metheny (including his thoughts on composing, improvising, and developing a unique style); and more! There are 167 songs in all!

00660000   Lead Sheets $49.99

PAT METHENY – TRIO 99-00
INCLUDES TAB
All 11 tracks from the 2000 release by Metheny, playing in a trio with bassist Larry Grenadier and drummer Bill Stewart. Includes: Capricorn • Giant Steps • A Lot of Livin' to Do • The Sun in Montreal • What Do You Want? • and more.

00690558   Guitar Recorded Versions $19.95

PAT METHENY TRIO – LIVE
INCLUDES TAB
13 selections from the release documenting the Trio's 2000 world tour: All the Things You Are • The Bat • Counting Texas • Faith Healer • Giant Steps • Into the Dream • James • Night Turns into Day • Soul Cowboy • Unity Village • and more.

00690561   Guitar Recorded Versions $22.95

PAT METHENY GROUP – THE WAY UP
This is the complete score for the four-part composition from this new release by the Pat Metheny Group. NPR says the album has "an ambitious compositional style that amounts to an epic journey."

00672541   Transcribed Scores............ $19.95

FOR MORE INFORMATION, SEE YOUR LOCAL MUSIC DEALER, OR WRITE TO:

HAL•LEONARD® CORPORATION
7777 W. BLUEMOUND RD. P.O. BOX 13819 MILWAUKEE, WI 53213

www.halleonard.com

Prices, contents, and availability subject to change without notice.
Prices listed in U.S. funds.